The Penguin Poets

Children of Albion

Poetry of the Underground in Britain

Michael Horovitz was born in Frankfurt, the youngest of ten children whose parents were descended from Rabbis. He came to London when he was two, went to various LCC schools, and read English at Oxford. He abandoned his projected B.Litt. thesis about the influence of Blake on Joyce and early in 1959 started *New Departures*, an international review of experimental work in all the arts. The present anthology is intended to reveal his subsequent ten years' involvement with the living poetry which he found all around, within and without him.

Michael Horovitz has exhibited paintings and collages in various galleries. His publications include *Europa*, a translation of the first Polish Futurist poem (1961; with Stefan Themerson), *Alan Davie*, a small monograph (1962), *Nude Lines* (1964), *Strangers* (poems, 1965), *Poetry for the People* (1966), *Bank Holiday* (1967), and a popular allegory of poet-readers as *The Wolverhampton Wanderer* (1969).

Poetry of the Underground in Britain

Children of Albion

Edited and Extradicted
by Michael Horovitz

Penguin Books

Penguin Books Ltd, Harmondsworth,
Middlesex, England
Penguin Books Inc., 7110 Ambassador Road,
Baltimore, Maryland 21207, U.S.A.
Penguin Books Australia Ltd, Ringwood,
Victoria, Australia

First published by Penguin Books 1969
Reprinted 1970
Copyright © Michael Horovitz, 1969
Afterwords copyright © Michael Horovitz, 1969

Made and printed in Great Britain by
Cox & Wyman Ltd, London, Reading and Fakenham
Set in Monotype Bembo

Contents

6 *Contents*

9 *Contents*

For Allen Ginsberg

Be kind to the heroes that have lost their
    names in the newspaper
and hear only their own supplication for
    the peaceful kiss of sex in the giant
    auditoriums of the planet,
nameless voices crying for kindness in the orchestra,
screaming in anguish that bliss come true
    and sparrows sing another hundred years
    to white haired babes
and poets be fools of their own desire – O Anacreon
    and angelic Shelley!
Guide these new-nippled generations on space
    ships to Mars' next universe
The prayer is to man and girl, the only
    gods, the only lords of Kingdoms of
    Feeling, Christs of their own
    living ribs –

(from 'Who Be Kind To', written for and read
at the first International Poetry Incarnation at the
Albert Hall in June 1965)

John Arden

Here I Come

John paddles up and down the long brown street
On two brown boats which are his two flat feet
And London houses blink at him and whisper:
'Whose are those spectacles, whose is that thin whisker?
Is he to be one who sees us as we are,
Stock-brick and concrete, mortar and tar,
Sees how we squat above an old green field
To choke its life? We are the iron shield
Screwed tight upon the buried face below:
John Arden sees us: we see him: we know.'

And how sadly his loud feet beat the ground:
'My lady lady, hear that hollow sound.
I'm stamping on a hollow skull, around
The skull a ring of gold, around the gold
A box of oak, around the oak a fold
Of heavy lead and round the lead the clay
Pressed by the houses tighter every day.
And so forth, lady. This is not your land:
It gives you no love. But you understand
The under-life my feet discover here.
You understand the houses and my fear
Between their rows of doorposts as I pass.'

So Arden hurries, pitying the grass
That fights the pavements hopelessly,
And round his ears his hair hangs raggedly.
His only golden crown lies fruitlessly,
Nailed to a bone, too deep for him to dig.

The Husband

The Sailor came home from the sea, as many a song will tell:
He wanted to live by the green trees on the green face of a hill.
He brought with him an outlandish wife both dangerous and
    proud,
You could tell her by her scaly tail from a hundred wives in a
    crowd.

She called herself by thirteen names. He knew her by but one.
The first time that she loved with him she had borne him a son.
The son was like a whiting-fish with his tail curled through his
    eye:
She looked at him with a frozen heart and said, Lay this one by.

She laid him on the river-strand when the tide was full in flood:
He floated out upon the ebb in a streak of silver blood.
She looked back at her sailor with the foam behind her ear
And he called her oh his lovely gull, his mackerel-heart so dear.

The next time that he loved with her he got no child at all,
So he tried the game again, he rode her for a fall,
She was his rearing water-horse and his bridle was so short
He swore that he had caught her and he held what he had
caught.

In time she bore another son and this was a raging bear;
He stood upon two timber legs and his arms were black with
    hair,
His nose was blunt as oakwood and his eyes were a charcoal
    glow
And round and round the hillside trees like a cannon-ball he
    would go.

The sailor said then to his wife, The first was from the sea,
But this one is a landward son and he belongs to me.
She stretched out pale upon her bed and the gate of her teeth
    shut-to:
She swore, I'll never have no more if they must be claimed by
    you.

But so: she smiled: she broke her oath: and she with young
    proved full.
She took herself all by herself to the edge of a seaweed pool,
And there she has her third brought forth and he was round and
    small
His body tight and prickly and rolled up in a ball.

Now was he, as she always said, an urchin-of-the-wave:
Or was he, as his father said, a hedgehog hard and grave?
We cannot know. So jealously she kept him in her care
That the sailor never could come at him, for all that he might
    dare.

I'll Make My Love a Breast of Glass

I'll make my love a breast of glass
And a heart of the porcelain white
The red blood seen through this clear window
Will stain it now dark now light.
I will make my love a head of gold
With hair of the black crow's feather
Her eyeballs of diamonds set therein
To crackle like thundery weather.

I'll make my love two arms of ice
Two hands of the rigid snow
I'll make my love two legs of flame
That will char the grass where they go.
I will make her a belly of the round moonlight
And the secret parts beneath
I will make of stars in a rainy night
Now hidden now gleaming like teeth.

To travel thereunder is my hope and my joy
To travel thereunder alone
An uncertain ride on a pitching road
Between black mire and sharp stone.
But what I will make, I will make and set up
In the corner of my love's crooked room
That she may regard it and learn from its shape
With what contrast of lust I consume.

I will make my love this image to love
And upon its hard brow I will write:
'This dream is my love yet you are my love
And who can tell which in the night?'
I will serve her in duty with flesh like an oak
And yet she will never know
How strong and how often I am serving the other
Stark naked in fire and in snow.

The Young Woman from Ireland

I was walking out
Upon this rainy day
A half-blind gay young woman
Came agreeably in my way

She travelled out of Ireland
Into England to live
To blink for a young Englishman
And her affection to give

'Oh I have had sorrows
I have had grief
So many men's sorrows
As the dew falls on the leaf

So many said they loved me
With words at my ears
Like needles of sharp ivory
They scraped me with their beards

So many said they loved me
And I blinked at them again
But all that they did for me
The wind does for the rain'

We were in Trafalgar Square
Where the rain was blown to hail
Lord Nelson's eye was filled with feathers
From every pigeon's tail

'I can half-see you, you young Englishman
And naked shall you stand
Between my white bosom
With your hand in my hand

If you want I can then clothe you
In red and in white
Your eyes in my bedroom
Shall be all I need for light'

Her eyes being weak and watery
She took liberty to use mine
She said, 'Where I could see three tall chimneys
Now I can see nine'

The eyes she borrowed from me
She returned to me once more
And I see a whole great waterscape
I never saw before

So I am rowing out today
On this rainy windy lake
That throws my boat so up and down
I am sure my oars will break.

Peter Armstrong

Butterfly

the butterfly it's
            a crazy toy
mechanical and
            wound up it goes
like a pub-crawler
            to the open throats of flowers.

Freight

The brave days of aviation!
            Saint-Exupery, delirious
poet of a night atmosphere
            turbulent and dangerous as black waves
fragmenting like safety-glass
            on Viking dragon heads
went back to it smiling.
            No camera unfortunately
to witness him huddled
            there in the shuddering cockpit
counting his chances
            with compass broken
and a sinking fuel meter,
            only his own wild prose
to recreate the fear, the sing
            of overstressed rigging wires.
But what photographs there are
            of similar frail aircraft

with grinning (thumbs up !) pilots
        wrestling them into the air
as if by their own muscle
        show often a taut windsock
as an emblem of brash confidence.

        Something, perhaps
the ambiguity of adrenaline,
        near love in watching
the wood and canvas wings
        shake as the motor
stuttered into life
        made such men seem fools:
Lindberg who watched red-eyed
        as the wrinkled Atlantic unrolled
for hours, too near
        while flying under a storm,
Parer and M'intosh who crashed
        their way from England to Australia,
arriving with one pint of petrol,
        Allcock and Brown, who
walked to an Irish village,
        their plane upended in a peat-bog . . .
The dreaming travellers
        slumped like mailbags
stir fretfully.
        Somewhere, a match flickers,
a cigarette, a cough.
        A sigh:
a shadow
        like a man with arms outstretched
in permanently drugged sleep
        passes over the earth,
many times
        as a matter of routine.

The Poppies

The poem is Eurydice.

Haiti, South Africa, the Congo,
Algeria, Hungary,
Vietnam: the prisoners stirring
like blind animals
in their own excrement.

Some nights
the labyrinthine dream
of Orpheus opens.
I get near understanding
but wake.

Reclined here, sunning myself,
the commonplace of a full belly
sags across my backbone.
It is summer. The cornfields
are full of poppies.

Be-Bop

tense over his saxophone
the brown man plays
jazz   no one has ever
been able to record this
accurately

it is a matter
of speaking   one voice
to many
against them

an American voice
terse and
interrupted
like talking into a telephone

a voice
talking in time
urgently

then breaking off.

Sometimes

the clouds become a profile
which disintegrates, as random images
come to mean something, you chase shadows,
knightwise the eye tries to follow them
through rectangles of prose.

It's all a butterfly
wired to a clown's cap, I think,
the cloud's grimace and prose alive
with off-centre eye defects.

How lucky then
that to some of us, a thing is a thing,
plain as a suet dumpling –
though wine and piss fall
equally in a parabola
and it's hard to tell sometimes.

Pete Brown

Few

Alone tired halfdrunk hopeful
I staggered into the bogs
at Green Park station
and found 30 written on the wall

Appalled I lurched out
into the windy blaring neon Piccadilly night
thinking surely,
Surely there must be more of us than that . . .

Reckless

Last night I was reckless –
didn't brush my teeth
and went to bed tasting
my dinner all night

And it tasted good

Job

Get a job, shouts my father.

A huge tank crawls from his mouth
Desperately I scream, I want cars with furry doors!

But it mows me down

Commemoration

Quick before my pencil wears down quick
about Sunday morning, well
All night wed sat I on the landing
outside the partyflat wed been thrown out of
reading poetry to whisky and you
going up and down crosslegged
in the lift talking to Singh
waving beer and Buddhism at him
who was Sikh and small and didnt drink,
and finally we drove across the Thames glaring
at its neonbanks glaring
to another party getting in by drink
and finding friends and jazz and beds and what more
and at dawn sausages in cut/loaf/slices
and tea not tea Tea,
then driving off getting high on day
beneath the vast mourning morning
of Battersea powerstation looming tombstone
in a shroud of smoke and the Sundaypaper advertisements
outside the stationers'
about the LAST DAYS OF THE BRITISH
IN INDIA later we all collapsed

Road

They tore up the old road
and buried it under a new one.
I didnt mind

£100

Suddenly I find £100 beneath a rock!
the Sky creeps
into my hand
I kiss the rocks and they turn golden
then uttering prayers
cut off both my thumbs

Scared

My neighbour and I
We are scared of each other

He is scared of my beard and I
am scared hell break
the fragile guyropes of
my tent with his car

Beautiful

Shes beautiful I suppose
I see her every evening
we pass each other on the cliff
she says nothing
and I say nothing
and she does not come from the Sea
She comes from Bristol

Dead

I suddenly think,
if youre not here youre dead
I imagine you
your face full of dead mirrors
a flower growing from your grey thighs,
laughing

Chorus 30 from *Blues for the Hitchhiking Dead*

The last of a gaggle of thirty newts
gigantic fourlegged brontoplanes
swims through the sky in a mass of bubbles
 & bursts on the sunpyre fire city
30 people on the beach before the impending sunmass
quail   melt into one in the heat   no trail
in the liquid sand only a sound of people praying
so a life is like a pebble over a cliff   except
this time the whole beach has fallen into the sea
 & the sea has fallen into the sky revealing to the eye
of no one but the sun a desert of skeleton galleoned trails
 & the paths of people like the slime of snails
glisten and disappear –

Slam

(*for Spike Hawkins*)

They slammed the door
in my face
I opened
the door in mv face

My father put me
to bed sneering
Youre a crossbreed
Its true, vinegar
was pouring from my ears & nostrils

When I got into bed
the walls swore
hideously all night long
and a hidden radio chanted
RENT A CHOCOLATE BISCUIT
FOR ONLY £30 A DAY,
THEYRE SLIMY AND COMFORTABLE!

Half-way through the
night I
went into the garden
and tried to hang
several ants with my bootlace

When I got back
the floor was covered
in bloody maps
and there was a live
octopus in the sink
trying to swallow a
record by Charlie Mingus

I started
sweeping up the
leaves embroidered on
the curtains undismayed
by the savagery next door
Someone hurled a spear
right through the wall
cutting last years calendar in 2

The next step was to
carry the electric stove
around trying to melt
the doorknobs
I achieved this
silently and
soon all the doors
were blazing merrily
Welcome inferno! I
shouted

They found me
in the kitchen
trying to outwhistle
the whistling kettle

In the morning my
mother
had me arrested
by 7
uniformed uncles
named Bloch

Vision

Wow! 2
small virgins
carrying
a gigantic
mattress!

Poet and Philosopher

Q: Can you hear the sound
     of the sun striking the ant?

A: No, Ive been pissed for three weeks.

Dreaming the Hours Away
(*Clarence Williams session 12 January 1928*)

I think of them in those rooms
whole corners of tuba shadow
clarinets/ the proud women envied their voices
– that wild old croaking beauty tenor,
silver gutturals of stop/time
majestic sweet with alto mixture   then
kind trombone even though
no mellow sun in this roomgloom

Piano of happy teeth banjo a negro moon
smoking a huge cigar
and the King black catnotes
river of fierce tight sound
no mute could ever check
All/
     down/
               the huge old horn
of recording tomorrow
Dreaming – dreaming the hours away
I think of them
in those old recording studios
I think of them
in those rooms

The Confidences

Due to her failure with him,
she told me; deeply moved,
I fell in love with her; she
then fell in love with my friend,
whom she met while visiting
me; I told my friend of
my failure with her, and
he assured me that he too
had been put off, as he dis-
trusted her love for being
too presumptuous; she meanwhile
was busy being infatuated
with his girlfriend, my former
girlfriend, who in a rash
moment told me of her failure
with him; panicking, I realized
I still loved her, despite
the past; while my former loves
old boyfriend, now sick of both
his lover, a 70-year-old Thurso
fisherman, and his psychiatrist,
desperately attempted anew
to rescale his former loves heights.
She, for her part, had for-
saken her bodily pursuits,
and had retired to a well appointed
hostel for antique asylum bed
collectors near Eastbourne; while
my friend had accidentally died
attempting to kill himself; in
the oppressive silence following
his death his girlfriend left

for the country,
an unspecified part shrouded in woods,
from which she did not re-emerge;
Griefstricken, I turned to writing,
realizing gleefully that nothing
mattered but the large jar full
of dead wasps by the window, from
summers ago; and in the space
that followed the disappearance
of most of their patients into
the fourth dimension and adjacent,
the voices of the frustrated psychiatrists
could still be heard, as though
in a desert, shouting confidential details
of the various case-histories
to each other, exultantly

Jim Burns

Negative

Sorting through a box full of old
wire, pencils, plugs, and so on,
I came across the roll of film.
Held it up to the light, and
there you were again, pulling
your face away from my lips; that
photo taken in a boat on the lake
at Munster, a few days after we
first met. Jock and his girl so
happy and in love, and you fresh
from a jilting, and taking it out
on me. It's over seven years ago
since that day, and five since I
last saw you; towards the end you'd
changed, and it was my turn to hold
back, letting you know that
I had you, and could make the tears
come with an idle threat. And now
I wonder what you're doing and where
you are, and I hold the film up
to the light again, making the
figures clear and alive once more,
and then return it to its place
amongst the bits and pieces that
have accumulated during the last
few years, and which only come to
my notice when I'm searching in vain
for something that I once discarded.

The End Bit

Each man has
his own way
of doing it.
Some take their
time, easing
out slowly,
and others
leave it late
and finish
with a jerk.
Neither of
these ways is
best, however,
and the man
who has no worries
about the
coming climax
is lucky,
and counts it
as part of the
pattern of things.

The Trouble with me is Irrelevancy

To have to
   get up
      in the morning
and go
   down there
      for money.

Right, let's rehearse it!

> No, wait while
> we think about
> what happened
> last night.
>   AH!

Ok, here we go.
>   Waking to find
my wife's behind pressed
>   against my thighs.

Right, let's rehearse that!
>   AH!

So, I still have
  to get up
    in the morning
and go
  down there
    for money.

Alright, let's concentrate at the point
where her behind is no longer pressed
against my thighs.

> The time is six, and we
> don't go to work until nine.
> She gives me some of hers,
> and I give her some of mine.

But still have
    to get up
        in the morning
and go
    down there
        for money.

Now this is what I'll do
                        when she
gets out of bed,
                    dressing herself in front
of me and slipping
                    everything on slowly,
so it looks good.

> ' *Takes a rocking chair to rock,*
> *rubber ball to roll,*
> *long tall baby*
> *to make my blood run cold*'*

And I still have
    to get up
        in the morning
and go
    down there
        for money.

But maybe now you'll understand
                                why
I lose so much of my pay
                        each week
through being late.

* Joe Turner – 'Sally Zu Zazz'

Johnny Byrne

Siege

he peeps   i duck
i shoot   he ducks
i wave   he waves back
i peep   he shoots
he waves   i shoot
and duck   i peep

i peep again

he's dead
                  draped across his turret
he smiles   my arrow tickles
the inside of his head

Charles Cameron

From *Chew Several Times*

buddha was a strange cat
wouldnt hurt a fly
but he used to pick flowers

*

    (perhaps its the weather
    perhaps im too tired)
theres something wrong with that tree
    (perhaps the next tree)

    the tree is imperfect
    (perfect)
theres not a thing wrong with that tree
    (splendid & faulty like me)

*

the moon must get tired
up all night
every night

*

the only unicorn
cant see itself anywhere
 & doesnt believe in unicorns

*

the dragon eats
not its tail only
but its own mouth even

*

the shortest distance
between you and me
is together

*

theres a beautiful moment
at the start of pain –
hold it there

*

cushions
are buddhas
who have been sitting here longer

*

aladdin
rubs his eyes
 & sees a stained glass window

David Chaloner

days
    long with fern shoots

        we embrace by
        streams
whose secrets educate
                    the
        pebbles
            banks necklaced
with hanging roots
            rinsed by the waters
flow
        in this tranquillity
        We hold allegiance
to no one

        our ears ripe
for the streams
        wisdom

*

don't misunderstand me

its not your beautiful
pear shaped breasts
or thighs soft as moss
pale as a winter moon

or lips red & moist
like wild berries
or belly scented with
roses
or hands mobile as
a flight of doves
or the dark chamber of
your sex

I hardly notice

lets be friends

*

asylum cringes in troubled sleep   organ dreams
boom along the ancient deserted corridors
      clocktower knocks out hell dispersing the stars
across a million million miles
            the binding silence cuts the ear &
hollow crys are lost in broken minds   songless
the night unsteady as an old film escapes
through freedoms keyhole   tears lay dust low as
the dead   tireless eyes watch   unblinking
crouched figures still as vacuums line the
halls
      the sound of weeping burns like acid
mice groan
            behind the skirting

*

coming to me as part of a pattern,
 & not remotely   ,   as one may expect:
            thus

finding myself , or being conscious
suddenly,
of my
surroundings:

small railway station
occupying its
relative length of
track beyond the
town,
noiseless in the solid heat:

ineffectual posters revealing
sunny southsea , brighton , eastbourne ,
or where ever , a guise
I never witnessed:
beauties smiling down
onto the perfunctory
soulless , platform:

here I waited an hour,
eating cheese:
the sun an obscure
glare,   roads shimmering ,
the yellow dandelions
dulled with a
layer of dust,

& all deserted . . . .

a strange elation at recollected events , long
filed in the memory: associations at the
sound of distant sea , the shouts of playing
children , a hens peaceful clucking:

kinship to what
man has labeled
insecure

Barry Cole

The Question

I noticed first a book had been exchanged.
The bible had gone, in its place a myth.
The children's paintings had been rearranged.
The brass alarm clock had been tampered with.
According to its hour hand I was late.
Why were there no children? Where had they gone?
Then the silence began to irritate.
They were much too young to be out alone.
I'd always thought of the carpet as red.
There wasn't the usual smell of cooking.
The only food about the place was bread.
I wondered what on earth she'd been doing.
A man in my chair held a glass of beer.
He looked up and said What are you doing here?

Reported Missing

Can you give me a precise description?
Said the policeman. Her lips, I told him,
Were soft. Could you give me, he said, pencil
Raised, a metaphor? Soft as an open mouth,
I said. Were there any noticeable
Peculiarities? he asked. Her hair hung
Heavily, I said. Any particular
Colour? he said. I told him I could recall
Little but its distinctive scent. What do
You mean, he asked, by distinctive? It had

The smell of a woman's hair, I said. Where
Were you? he asked. Closer than I am to
Anyone at present, I said; level with
Her mouth, level with her eyes. Her eyes?
He said. What about her eyes? There were two,
I said, both black. It has been established,
He said, that eyes cannot, outside common
Usage, be black; are you implying that
Violence was used? Only the gentle
Hammer blow of her kisses, the scent
Of her breath, the . . .   Quite, said the policeman,
Standing. But I regret that we know of
No one answering to such a description.

John Cotton

Tiger Caged

The tiger treads his cage.
400 lbs of muscle, bone
And thwarted purpose rage.

The sun shines through cage bars
On his barred coat the sun,
His tiger sun,
Shines through.

He does not look
At those who look at him.
They are without
The cage he treads within.

From what the bars divide
The side you are depends.
Each has his bars,
His limits and his ends.

The tiger treads his cage.
400 lbs of muscle, bone
And thwarted purpose rage.

Pumpkins

At the end of the garden,
Across the litter of weeds and grass cuttings
The pumpkin spreads its coarse,
Bristled, hollow-stemmed lines,
Erupting in great leaves
Above flowers
The nobbly and prominent
Stigmas of which
Are like fuses
Waiting to be set by bees.

When, like a string
Of yellow mines
Across the garden,
The pumpkins will smoulder
And swell,
Drawing their combustion from the sun
To make their own.

At night I lie
Waiting for detonations,
Half expecting
To find the garden
Cratered like a moon.

Andrew Crozier

What Spokes, & To What Hub?

There are many parts I have not been to, but start
from Gloucester, coming from Fishguard that morning, and
                                                    [eventually
from Courtmacsherry, leaving in a rainstorm on the afternoon
                                                    [bus
thirty miles north to Cork to take the night ferry
                                        walked that
morning into Haverfordwest, only council lorries on the road
carrying earth to some site off the main route
            a manifest regret
                        a short way
out of town with a travelling grocer, a fine thing to be
a poet, his son at Cardiff training to be an engineer
                                    fast to Cardigan
I could only buy ice creams   and walk out of the town
a deep valley where the road branches east and
north to Lampeter, rain and more Council works
I rode a lorry from there a week before
coming south from the Williams's at Llandecwyn nr. Talsarnau
                        I follow east
towards London, my home
with a traveller making for Devon
the next night, so far around the Bristol Channel
we swung south towards Cardiff on a call, his day's
work, then I brought him back north
across the Carmarthenshire mountains, the Brecon Beacons
high grasslands where no one lives, no sheep are grazed even
                        a quorn the size of a mill wheel

                    is lost there
                    Yvor Pritchard my father's friend
                    went back and could not find it
        a proximate horizon   the hills arch
a narrow sky you climb steadily towards
back to the main route, turning east to
run through the little marcher towns, Brecon, Monmouth
past a signpost: To Usk
                              ten miles away
I could stop and turn down there, easily
find a family in a town of 2,000, know at least
where she went
but that was sixteen months ago, and I did not stop, it is
even further away as I remember her
in Brighton, spending Easter at Kimbo's place
and it snowed as I came through Redhill
Was it she came to these States this summer? to ride to Los
                                                    [Angeles
her name, her gesture, her age
            I know one her like now –
            is there attraction in resemblance?
I rode on to Gloucester

A Day, A Garden, Stay Awake to Dream

I was tired and lass-
itude lay over me as I
lay on the bed. What got me up
and to the table
was to write this. Enough
to get me on my feet, to sit here
with damp hair and wanting to go to sleep.

I have done nothing today
(that's a euphemism) but arrange for a job
I begin tomorrow, and on my way home
look at some tropical plants and smell
the delight of liquid fertilizer. In a dull narration
I feel dull, and passed my hand over my face
as I noticed reflected in the window.
There the lilac blooms
stand out of the darkness, I tell their colour
and from it the green of leaves. The mass moves
in the wind, and is the opposite of dense.
I never found a word for that. It moves as
in a denser medium, as to the incoming tide
the anemone unfurls and sways.
The lilac's sweetness
doesn't penetrate, yet by night
the tobacco plant blooms sweetest. I am awakening
to this green life, infer, and find
a hand across my eyes and a chill strike
across my shoulders and constrict my sides.
It's panic. My dreams have been
of torture and rejection, and I awoke sweating
wondering at the source of the finished image.
What can I know of torture? Then tonight I saw
americans practising on each other
in a t.v. picture. It was formal, but I think
of an informal daily torture. A man was screaming
in the street drunk on meths and it crept
cold beneath my skin. To one another
we are cold and it is metaphor
as it is physiology and I am
afraid. A body's touch
is warmth
and I am not afraid
afterwards

Pidgin on the Lorne

Wots this a dirt blew
pidgin doin on owr lorne
warking up and down amung
the sparras peckin the bred
and stum-bling in its hayst.
Hay grate big piggin pidgin
flap off yewr frite-ning my birds.
See theres wun chaste up a rows bush
stem yew coodent stand sidewise on
wun yewr too big for my garding
fat bird and spoyl the scayl.

Compliments from the French

They both said How about that Welsh girl
you were with then? and at first
I thought Is she? How can they tell?
But I remember one or two I've known
like you, tall and strutting
all nose and black hair. I'll grin
again and say You know the sort! Grand girls!

In Pontypool said Dave he said It's all right
him fucking my wife while I'm on night shift
I'm getting his while he's on days. And
how well his Grandad was hung to the admiring women
around the tin bath before the kitchen grate.
Aren't you lucky, May, that's finer
than's on my Bryn! Yes said Cliff
that's how it should be. Oh said Dave
I donno.

Blown into a Corner

In her head
   a pain
      or memory

her mouth
   cannot move to
      that gesture
of love

who is bashful
   was not
      an hour before

hides her face
   hand over mouth
      in the pillow

something there
   not to do
      with who is
there by her

inserts the past
   against the present
      who knows

enough
   to help himself

Dave Cunliffe

Night Book of the Mad

3am & my alarm clock has crawled into the wall.
The eyelids of the moon are silent & sleeping now.

Too soon to fill in the pages of my report.

Let's see . . . 'patients & staff slept throughout the
night' or 'Peter had a weird fit but we fixed
him with paraldehyde & his own fantasies.'

No, better not . . . 'nothing special to report' . . .
that'll do for now to fill these tired pages.

Maybe 10 shit-ups & a corpse is a record for summer.

Night softens the cold shrouds & pale lips of
these long & bitter dormitories & suspends their agony.

I've still got to butter the bread & dress the cripples.
Too long bored with filling in this night book.

'64 patients & 32 empty beds on my last patrol.'
'This couch is torn, stinks & requires fixing.'

Truth devours all in this sad & terrible world.
10 shit-ups & a corpse is surely a record.

'Thompson N expired after an unconsummated bowel action.'

Outside thick rain crucifies the trembling fingers of
stars & within these walls legs erupt & wither in spasms.

It is now time to fill in my morning report for
in the night book of the mad all is poetry.

Who Are the Angels?

You are poised above us with your ego & your
rumours of the last days & we stand naked &
vulnerable; eager for agony & humiliation.
How long have we awaited the mythical assassin
who will free us from obedience & radiation?

Humble my wife; her deep eyelids of sleep.
Humble the cretin with his bruised smile.

Each moment exploding within her thighs; a sign
 & each sign heralding a world of joy forever.
Do not preach for the preacher oft dies as he
flees; guilt stains splayed upon his shadow.
The moon grows old & now the sky is weeping.

Ugly the squat black gun streaked with oil.
Ugly the unwashed wound encrusted with grime.

We extract the white bullet from inbetween your eyes.
Your eyes swell & envelop dead stars drifting through
skies thick with charred torn abandoned wings.
Who are the angels who shot down God & left a
clean bloodless hole in our, & the worlds, imagination?

The Awfully Nice Young Man

There's some things I just don't understand.
Like the time that beautiful young lady
entered a train carriage & took off all
her clothes;   cupped those firm young

breasts in both hands;   stuck out a
fine white arse;   bristled her deep black
pubic hairs;   stroked a soft moist
cunt;   laid back & stretched those long
lovely legs out wide & invitingly. . . .
 & the only man in that compartment
threw down his paper,   leapt to his
feet, & draped his overcoat around her.

The lifes & deaths of a whore

They have filed slowly through your life & have
tasted the taut parched skin of your wasted body;
gleaming softly in the night as they entered you.

They did not see your nude bruised thighs
thresh stupidly on chill dirt floors; faintly
moist with stale urine; wine seeping slowly through
thick brown blankets & thin love stained sheets.

You have died young, without love, &
your grim tragedy is that those who
have tendered to your needs, & we who
have watched you die, do not even care.

A letter to a few good poets I know

Guns are made of steel & wood but the
wondrous giver of life is flesh between your legs.
Your future is ever fused with the beauty without
for it knows no form other than the creating &
making of things & the gentle nourishing of life.

History saw many cruel leaders, vast armies,
slaughtered peoples, much suffering & grim death.
You must each free yourself from leaders,
passports, territories, & all barriers which
seek to divide, & grow as new free men
amongst us; the mad patriot forever destroyed.
You must warn of the cancer of money & greed,
the politician, mercenary, judge, hangman &
censor; the terrible prophet messenger of death.
You who must embrace the men & women of
love, tolerance & peace; the makers of life.

O Come Love These Warring Armies

Come join in the angels naked march.
Each bearing truly special gifts of
precious fruit, prayer-beads, love-chimes,
wooden dolls & brightly coloured masks.

O come love these savage warring armies
& scatter rose-petals upon their tanks.

Come carrying giant mandala banners,
inscribed with messages of universal love.
Chanting endless mantric poems & softly
beating drums with gentle mudra fingers clasped.

O come love these fearful warring armies
& plant tulips deep inside their guns.

Come ready armed with flowers, bibles, buddhas
& protect each other with kindly thoughts.
Seek out each aggressor to invite him to
smoke with you the magic weed of peace.

O come love these trembling warring armies
& drop upon them tender psychedelic bombs.

Some folks seem to go through hell without gain

There was this old lama, a good kindly man, proudly sitting
in the marketplace telling his beads & some idiot
muledriver had just happened to pocket one the previous night.

Well to get to the sad point, the poor guy couldn't
figure out what was wrong & kept on starting again.

No matter how we struggle, persevere & attain
Somebody comes along to foul up the works.

Milarepa kept on building mighty castles & beautiful
monasteries & as soon as they were finished Marpa knocked
    em down.

Milarepa learnt this lesson the hard way & when he accidentally
broke the pot he cooked his nettle dinner in he didn't cry.

That old lama still sat there in the very same place
scratching his head & counting his beads & looking grim.

Felix de Mendelssohn

In Praise of Hashish

[*Patio Tetuani, Tangier: August 1963*]

my eyes are doors

the moon walks through them

i have the moon in my head
it is white   round   luminous
as they say
                it is heavy

my skin is cut to pieces
   by the sharp points of the stars

my body is polarized
hangs
              has an orbit
rotates.
         My body is earth.

              The sea under my window
                   laps at my throat

       (the doors are closed . . .

there is a new moon in the sky

the moon in the sky
 & the moon in my head
look at each other
                    there is

                          silence

The Alchemist Addresses His Friends Part Two

(*for Olivia de Haulleville*)

yes I hung up those luminous nets in the sky today
to wander under, catching myself
sometimes by a black tower in thought
of the mysteries of the Egg, and how it would end.

I would not join the Patrol though the cafés
were beginning to boil red at last, trusting
the Sun God would guide my fingers through the afternoon

yes I laid out what you (perhaps) see those
leaning traceries of light wire which I find
my way along the edges   /   I am not certain
just how the next foot
will fall I am still
the Interpreter. These places just inside of time
are open; knowing them
is to feel an uneasy wonder, as though
a strange wind had blown across your face.

Batucada Fantastica

tonight one man standing motionlessly in the courtyard
his hair goes white in a day
is it me?
this is it now – the drums will throw
any age at you, if you let it stick

   'Señor, the world is mad'
we can make sense only of small slices
yes through the drums you can forget
everything, with the drums
   you can remember everything

        the trees growing like glad flags
           from the roof of the bombed ruins (munich
        war museum)
                        – a powerful dream
           cancels its own ticket –

you can start with anything, the history
     of beer   (in rivers, flowing
     from fields & sun through centuries)
or my 10 years in the jungle teaching the Ape
        to hang signs of life
        through the broken window
           & not to have foreseen the appearance of children
              like a bright plague, burning up the pattern

        clicking along old conveyor run
        by accident, faces backfiring
           from forgotten pockets, my pin-up girl
              discovered Now in the banana

I have saved a sweet moment exactly:
the white tennisplayer in a frozen leap
          over the net   :   his opponent
is up a tree – invisible, in the water –
          is perhaps why it sticks

          the drums teaching a mesh
          of hopeless knots & fragile threads
     strung out over the kaleidoscope courtyard
          The colours flash & change
                    from the fields & mellow rivers, the air
          fractures in a summer spectrum

 & the beerbottle in the sun's
a tough thing, could last three times
my lifetime

          if I let it –

My back to the Big Clock get lost in the Amazon

          & my hair at noon
                    turns white & black
                    & white.

Raymond Durgnat

Scrap Iron

A black steel carcass in a field of sheep
Repels the drench of light and weeps out rust
Lamenting gulped-up roads, the hedgerows smeared and
    blurred,
The bucking bridges and the startled birds.

The slow sap struggles to the screaming sun,
The lark upspirals on her simple song;
My spring is broken and my winter long,
This cold steel slowly burns to be a gun.

Paul Evans

The Peach

She cut the ripe peach
leaving a hollow
where the red sun had slept

I eased my tongue in
like a knife
sliding into the soft throat

and flowed down
on the sweet juices

Factory Incident & Revelation

Tipping the beer-crate, endways,
I shook out
the neck of a bottle. It
gashed my finger and
fell to the ground.

I didn't recognize, that time,
the animal peering
from behind the machinery,
the fur standing up
along its spine.

The Musicians
(*after Hieronymus Bosch*)

The players of instruments are naked, they
lie on their backs, pierced by the screams
of revellers in Hell.
                    One of them
carries a huge flute, one is condemned
to a music of farting, one is chained
to the neck of his lute.

They have no audience. The revellers
won't applaud them, pursued by
lust for money, their hearts torn out
by dogs.

A Song of My Country
(*for my wife*)

your back
your white rock in the dark
your smoothness of stone
not water has smoothed it
not wind
                    my hands
my fingers walk on the hill
my mouth follows
my animal feeds on you
                    your rock was never black
                    as my tongue
                    with hunger

my animal feels its way round you
and casts its shadow
on the slope
                    far down
in valley
            in deep water
it comes to rest

My Garden
(*for nasty children everywhere*)

The plants in my garden
make noises
                    at night. From the 2nd floor
I hear them.
                    They enter my dreams:

the red and white gladioli clank like railway waggons
dragged on chains;
the lawn paces its own length, again and again –
it will enter soon and climb the stairs,
the small stones rattling behind it;
I hear the lime tree turn over,
the sheets crackling with starch;
further away, but approaching,
a low hum from the bed of hydrangeas –
their heads appear at the window, whistling.

                    Below,
the lawn has stopped pacing and stands,
rubbing its hands and grinning . . .

                    I wake, and turn over
into the arms of the lime.

T—CA—C

The Intruder

You are sitting alone,
                    in quiet
                            at night –
a head of blue
              appears at the window,
                                    waving
                    as if on a stem.
It turns to go
              and you see
                          its body of metal
                                          shining
                          behind it.
                                  You
shout out a warning but
                        it turns and
                                    falls back
into whatever it was
                    you were reading.

The Hierarchies of Sound

Just the slightest
clink of a cinder
        in the fire
        dying down
woke my mind. I was reading
        a poem where
        the poet says
'it was the sound of a fire
on the hearth . . . sparks
        of delight.'

                    It woke me
and flared to a memory,
where I was sitting
        by the Thames
        at Chiswick Eyot,
                        listening

to the clink
        of a rusty tin
        scraping the shore,
pushed in
        by a ripple
        on a ripple. The scrape

of metal on stone
woke me to the
hierarchies of sound. Sparks
        of delight!

                A gull flew
into midstream from the shore,
wingtips hitting the water,
        a heavy sound.

I was listening
to the sound of the fire
        in a poem
when the clink of a cinder –
or was it a tin? –
plunged me in the silence
        of the river.

Out of Unrest

The blue iris, opening at dawn,
startled me out of my mind.
I turned

          away from it
          to the window:

     blue stars burning down,
     lighting the universe
     a moment, then dying
     into the sun's greater light.

*

Light that is reaching us from stars,
dead a thousand years, was held once
in the huge arms of Andromeda. We see
only memories of starfire – our bodies,
a memory of fathers long dead.
Their voices rush, muffled by distance,
down streams of the blood, opening channels
of first feeling in the flood.

*

     What piece of us is not
     striving to get back
     to the One Man, is dead.
     Who does not know the
     dead in the wind and
     the dead within would be one
     has no way out of time . . .

'. . . it does not really exist
without unrest; it does not exist
for dumb animals.' (Kierkegaard)

But I will not be dumb
nor rest, but celebrate
        what I am.

It is difficult. There are
so many people I am,
        obscuring

the one face I would become.

Ian Hamilton Finlay

The Dancers Inherit the Party

When I have talked for an hour I feel lousy –
Not so when I have danced for an hour:
The dancers inherit the party
While the talkers wear themselves out and
      sit in corners alone, and glower.

Orkney Interior

Doing what the moon says, he shifts his chair
Closer to the stove and stokes it up
With the very best fuel, a mixture of dried fish
And tobacco he keeps in a bucket with crabs

Too small to eat. One raises its pincer
As if to seize hold of the crescent moon
On the calendar which is almost like a zodiac
With inexplicable and pallid blanks. Meanwhile

A lobster is crawling towards the clever
Bait that is set inside the clock
On the shelf by the wireless – an inherited dried fish
Soaked in whisky and carefully trimmed

With potato flowers from the Golden Wonders
The old man grows inside his ears.
Click! goes the clock-lid, and the unfortunate lobster
Finds itself a prisoner inside the clock,

An adapted cuckoo-clock. It shows no hours, only
Tides and moons and is fitted out
With two little saucers, one of salt and one of water
For the lobster to live on while, each quarter-tide,

It must stick its head through the tiny trapdoor
Meant for the cuckoo. It will be trained to read
The broken barometer and wave its whiskers
To Scottish Dance Music, till it grows too old.

Then the old man will have to catch himself another lobster.
Meanwhile he is happy and takes the clock
Down to the sea. He stands and oils it
In a little rock pool that reflects the moon.

Roy Fisher

Why They Stopped Singing

They stopped singing because
They remembered why they had started

Stopped because
They were singing too well

When they stopped they hoped for
A silence to listen into.

Had they sung longer
The people would not have known what to say.

They stopped from the fear
Of singing for ever

They stopped because they saw the rigid world
Became troubled

Saw it begin
Composing a question.

Then they stopped singing
While there was time.

The Entertainment of War

I saw the garden where my aunt had died
And her two children and a woman from next door;
It was like a burst pod filled with clay.

A mile away in the night I had heard the bombs
Sing and then burst themselves between cramped houses
With bright soft flashes and sounds like banging doors;

The last of them crushed the four bodies into the ground,
Scattered the shelter, and blasted my uncle's corpse
Over the housetop and into the street beyond.

Now the garden lay stripped and stale: the iron shelter
Spread out its separate petals around a smooth clay saucer,
Small, and so tidy it seemed nobody had ever been there.

When I saw it, the house was blown clean by blast and care:
Relations had already torn out the new fireplaces;
My cousin's pencils lasted me several years.

And in his office notepad that was given me
I found solemn drawings in crayon of blondes without dresses;
In his lifetime I had not known him well.

Those were the things I noticed at ten years of age;
Those, and the four hearses outside our house,
The chocolate cakes, and my classmates' half-shocked envy.

But my grandfather went home from the mortuary
And for five years tried to share the noises in his skull;
Then he walked out and lay under a furze-bush to die.

When my father came home from identifying the daughter
He asked us to remind him of her mouth.
We tried. He said 'I think it was the one.'

These were marginal people whom I had met only rarely,
And the end of the whole household meant that no grief was
    seen.
Never have people seemed so absent from their own deaths.

This bloody episode of four whom I could understand better
    dead
Gave me something I needed to keep a long story moving;
I had no pain of it; can find no scar even now.

But had my belief in the fiction not been thus buoyed up,
I might, in the sigh and strike of the next night's bombs
Have realized a little what they meant, and for the first time
    been afraid.

Toyland

Today the sunlight is the paint on lead soldiers
Only they are people scattering out of the cool church

And as they go across the gravel and among the spring streets
They spread formality: they know, we know, what they have
                        been doing,

The old couples, the widowed, the staunch smilers,
The deprived and the few nubile young lily-ladies,

And we know what they will do when they have opened the
                        doors of their houses and walked in:
Mostly they will make water, and wash their calm hands and
                        eat.

The organ's flourishes finish; the verger closes the doors;
The choirboys run home, and the rector goes off in his motor.

Here a policeman stalks, the sun glinting on his helmet-crest;
Then a man pushes a perambulator home; and somebody posts
                        a letter.

If I sit here long enough, loving it all, I shall see the
                        District Nurse pedal past,
The children going to Sunday School and the strollers strolling;

The lights darting on in different rooms as night comes in;
And I shall see washing hung out, and the postman delivering
                        letters.

I might by exception see an ambulance or the fire brigade
Or even, if the chance came round, street musicians (singing
                        and playing).

For the people I've seen, this seems the operation of life:
I need the paint of stillness and sunshine to see it that way.

The secret laugh of the world picks them up and shakes them
                        like peas boiling;
They behave as if nothing happened; maybe they no longer
                        notice.

I notice. I laugh with the laugh, cultivate it, make much of it,
But I still don't know what the joke is, to tell them.

The Hospital in Winter

A dark bell leadens the hour,
        The three o'clock
Light falls amber across a tower.

Below, green-railed within a wall
        Of coral brick,
Stretches the borough hospital

Monstrous with smells that cover death,
        White gauze tongues,
Cold-water-pipes of pain, glass breath,

Porcelain, blood, black rubber tyres;
        And in the yards
Plane-trees and slant telephone-wires.

On benches squat the afraid and cold
        Hour after hour.
Chains of windows snarl with gold.

Far off, beyond the engine-sheds,
        Motionless trucks
Grew ponderous, their rotting reds

Deepening towards night; from windows
        Bathrobed men
Watch the horizon flare as the light goes.

Smoke whispers across the town,
        High panes are bleak;
Pink of coral sinks to brown;
A dark bell brings the dark down.

Starting to Make a Tree

First we carried out the faggot of steel stakes; they varied in length, though most were taller than a man.

We slid one free of the bundle and drove it into the ground, first padding the top with rag, that the branch might not be injured with leaning on it.

Then we took turns to choose stakes of the length we wanted, and to feel for the distances between them. We gathered to thrust them firmly in.

There were twenty or thirty of them in all; and when they were in place we had, round the clearing we had left for the trunk, an irregular radial plantation of these props, each with its wad of white at the tip. It was to be an old, downcurving tree.

This was in keeping with the burnt, chemical blue of the soil, and the even hue of the sky which seemed to have been washed with a pale brownish smoke;

another clue was the flatness of the horizon on all sides except the north, where it was broken by the low slate or tarred shingle roofs of the houses, which stretched away from us for a mile or more.

This was the work of the morning. It was done with care, for we had no wish to make revisions;

we were, nonetheless, a little excited, and hindered the women at their cooking in our anxiety to know whose armpit and whose groin would help us most in the modelling of the bole, and the thrust of the boughs.

That done, we spent the early dusk of the afternoon gathering materials from the nearest houses; and there was plenty:

a great flock mattress; two carved chairs; cement; chicken-wire; tarpaulin; a smashed barrel; lead piping; leather of all kinds; and many small things.

In the evening we sat late, and discussed how we could best use them. Our tree was to be very beautiful.

Experimenting

Experimenting, experimenting,
        with long damp fingers twisting
        all the time and in the dusk
White like unlit electric bulbs she said
'This green goes with this purple,' the hands going,
The question pleased: 'Agree?'

Squatting beside a dark brown armchair just round
        from the fireplace, one hand on a
        coalscuttle the other prickling across
        the butchered remains of my hair,
I listen to the nylon snuffle in her poking hands,
Experimenting, experimenting.
'Old sexy-eyes,' is all I say.

So I have to put my face into her voice, a
        shiny baize-lined canister
        that says all round me, staring in:
'I've tried tonight. This place!' Experimenting. And I:
'The wind off the wallpaper blows your hair bigger.'

Growing annoyed, I think, she clouds over, reminds me
        she's a guest, first time here, a comparative
        stranger, however close; 'Doesn't *welcome* me.'
        She's not young, of course;
Trying it on, though, going on about the milk bottle, table-leg,
The little things. Oh, a laugh somewhere. More words.
She knows I don't *live* here.

Only a little twilight is left washing around outside,
        her unease interfering with it as I watch.
Silence. Maybe some conversation. I begin:
'Perhaps you've had a child secretly sometime?'

'Hm?' she says, closed up. The fingers start again,
        exploring up and down and prodding,
        smoothing. Carefully
She asks 'At least – why can't you have more walls?'
Really scared. I see she means it.

To comfort her I say how there's one wall each, they
        can't outnumber us, walls, lucky to have the
        one with the lightswitch, our situation's better
        than beyond the backyard, where indeed the earth
        seems to stop pretty abruptly and not restart;
Then she says, very finely:
'I can't look,' and 'Don't remind me,' and 'That blue gulf'.

So I ask her to let her fingers do the white things again
        and let her eyes look and her hair blow bigger,
        all in the dusk deeper and the coloured stuffs
        audible and odorous;
But she shuts her eyes big and mutters:
                'And when the moon with horror –
                And when the moon with horror –
                And when the moon with horror' –

So I say 'Comes blundering blind up the side tonight.'
She: 'We hear it bump and scrape.'
I: 'We hear it giggle.' Looks at me,
'And when the moon with horror,' she says.

Squatting beside a dark brown armchair just round
            from the fireplace, one hand on a
            coalscuttle the other prickling across
            the butchered remains of my hair,
'What have you been reading, then?' I ask her,
Experimenting, experimenting.

Report on August

How do I sleep? Well, but
the dreams are bad:

filled with accusations
small but just.

These slack summer dawns
that fail of sunrise

There's a relief at falling
awake and into comfort,

becoming once again
four people, watching

from pillow level
my boys' khaki heads bustle about:

over breakfast I see,
staring at the garden,

how the times have fed;
under heavy leaves and low sky

in profile the bold woodpigeon
walks the lawn

Beats of a shadowy fanblade
tick through from behind,

time going; ignored,
nobody measuring time, so much

constant, the weather unchanging,
the work I do filling days

so that they seem one day,
a firm framework, made

of the window where I sit
(or lie, slumped, feet on the desk,

waved to by passers-by
like a paraplegic)

a window-shaped guise of myself
that holds what few events come round

like slides, and in what seems
capricious sequence.

Harry Guest

Samuel Beckett, 1961

A crocus flashes from the darkness. Trapped
in the mud spread-eagled the hero conjures
up yesterdays. Without too much screaming. That's
the way things are. What consolation? Simply

the occasional gag – though the grinding humour's fading –
an illusory blaze of grace from time to time;
each agonizing vision always then.
A white gate somewhere – a tramp without his trousers –

remember – a boat moored where the water shines.
Hang on to detail. Peer. That saves the moment.
Get out the tin-opener. Feel. Count the marbles.
Mortality is all we've got. The gag

in the darkness or the crocus. Nothing else.
Nowhere to get to. That's the way things are.

From *Private View*

Section IX

The image at the speed of light
Traverses air and eyeball, hits
The brain to splay and dissipate
And fade.
       Hard body to hard body. Scalp
On fire: cold blond, my sort of love,
A restricted flame. My hand's forbidden to ignite.

Externalize in colour. Freeze the muscle.
Now has turned into then and cheats.

The agony to see them walking
In a garden of other flowers.
                              You,
Blond, like a throw of gulls, casually
Perfect. Gone. Mine no longer although of course
Mine never.
On a windburnt cliff which the sea licked
A seabird, white, cut out on the blue,
Hung in the screaming air a hand away.
Immense and dangerous as that dizzy fall
Is the gap between my finger-ends and you.

Paint that. Depict that postage-stamp of sky
Which separates us as significant.
Get into empty space a sense of dynamite,
So nothing contains a spark to set the brain on fire.

Another glass? The wine trembles.
I sip and peer. After all, this is a Private View.
To shake the mind into a new awareness.

A window opens on to an unexciting orchard.
The trees flare. Apples burst and catherine wheels
Twirl and dazzle along the spars of trees.

When does the pen hit the paper?
Can recollection hit it off?
Must poems lag behind experience?

The king grins from his envelope of metal.

I look across the room again
And my throat contracts.
Whole translucent years of peace
Span the interval before I swallow.
Watching your brushed blond hair go dull
My fingers wither from the nail.
        Between your leg and my appalling hand,
A tactile section of room, stiff as dried oil paint,
Separates my stillborn sunrise –
A charred landscape and level white light –
From your impossible midday.

A few birds of prey go into the fresh sky.

Noon.
And see the dream for what it's worth;
Love-making in absentia.

A shaft of sunlight
Illuminates your cold head of hair.

It's only a picture.
This blue tree bending with a harsh light in its branches
Becomes a mast, we're off, rooted to the linoleum,
To an Eldorado. No escape.
No frivolity. Release into awareness.
Equate the Alltag here not with this room,
But with absence of significance.

And always the anguish. These huddled objects,
Light dropped on them from above,
Suggest unease. A ripple runs through the saucepan –
A lack of security drifts about these onions –
Angst at the sink.

And an infinite distance always there
Between the quiet hand and the mad self
That churns inside the jigsaw of toothed bone:
Between the surely not ambiguous canvas
And the blurred eye.

I sit at the table and the light leaves the coast.
At Broadstairs I write about rain over Nafplion.
Dressed and alone apart from the buzz of the electric fire
I start to analyse a Saturday of love.
Am I on life's side?
There has to be a time-lag but
Poetry must not be a substitute.
Not reportage but not escape.
Better perhaps to leave experience alone,
Remember the moment has its uses and
Never attempt the serio-comic business
Of trying to cohere on paper, do
A cold unhappy vaudeville turn
For an unseen few.
Humour is after all what we're outside of,
Once you start fearing what you're doing's funny,
There's an end to involvement, there's
The doppelgänger's face
In winter passionately dark
Beyond the pane.
And perhaps the gas oven.
Or, if not that, bitterness in the lung
And a scream of fury in answer to
All music, however personal.

Desire lifts up in absence
And the pen's unscrewed.
The nag, the phallic loneliness, once you're gone.

Sterility and regret are the only muse
Plus an anger at what we call injustice.
Injustice of choice, injustice of orgasm,
Injustice of the letter that doesn't arrive
When meaningless envelopes go on littering the hall,
Injustice of the one stabbing letter that does arrive,
Injustice when a request of twilight
Is answered by the electric light switch,
Injustice of marriage, injustice of false teeth,
Injustice of the knock on the door that interrupts,
Injustice of the poem no one wants to read,
Injustice of this crowd that keeps me from you,
Injustice of a different reaction,
Injustice of the often far too slow
Realization what is love, injustice
That being born you have to die
And being human you have to feel desire
More times than the year and your own face allow.

Lee Harwood

sciencefic

what if this big orange planet
met a soft blue planet?
their fur sides caressing one another
space peaches.
let me be at the meeting point.
death in a mink coat
laughing.
and kissing you.

for d.s.h.

No – all the temple bells
can only kneel
groans and chantings

a purity neither lost nor found
only a further dumbness with words

I can kneel here
            with no special ritual
but my own
a carpet design
            or a twisted heap of metal
my obsession god this minute

cymbals dulled drums
        my clothing so ornate that
        I have to move with ceremony
    gold and silver
        silks in my throat
a minute explosion puffing
from a small top window

whoever you are
let me shelter you

        and with this
        drumming rhythms grew
    until the entire planet was woven
                into

an elaborate stringball
rolling across a green desert
whose orange and humid night
I now eat and offer you

'let us reconsider . . . . . I mean these
mountain problems'
a car starting in a quiet side street

As your eyes are blue . . .

As your eyes are blue
you move me – & the thought of you –
I imitate you.
& cities apart yet a roof grey with slates
or lead the difference is little
& even you could say as much
through a foxtail of pain   even you

when the river beneath your window
was as much as I dream of. loose change &
your shirt on the top of a chest-of-drawers
a mirror facing the ceiling & the light in a cupboard
left to burn all day   a dull yellow
probing the shadowy room   'what was it?'

'cancel the tickets' – a sleep talk
whose horrors razor a truth that can
walk with equal calm through palace rooms
chandeliers tinkling in the silence as winds batter the gardens
outside   formal lakes shuddering at the sight
of two lone walkers
                              of course this exaggerates
small groups of tourists appear & disappear
in an irregular rhythm of flowerbeds

you know even in the stillness of my kiss
that doors are opening in another apartment
on the other side of town   a shepherd grazing
his sheep through a village we know
high in the mountains the ski slopes thick with summer flowers
 & the water-meadows below with narcissi
the back of your hand & –

a newly designed red bus drives quietly down Gower Street
a brilliant red   'how could I tell you . . .'
with such confusion
                              meetings disintegrating
 & a general lack of purpose only too obvious
in the affairs of state
                              'yes, it was on a hot july day
with taxis gunning their motors on the throughway
a listless silence in the backrooms of paris bookshops
why bother   one thing equal to another

dinner parties whose grandeur stops all conversation

but
         the afternoon sunlight which shone in
your eyes as you lay beside me watching for . . . –
we can neither remember – still shines as you
wait nervously by the window for the ordered taxi
to arrive   if only I could touch your naked shoulder
now   'but then . . . . .'

 & the radio still playing the same
records I heard earlier today
                              – & still you move me
 & the distance is nothing
'even you –

Summer

these hot afternoons 'it's quite absurd' she whispered
sunlight stirring her cotton dress inside the darkness when
an afternoon room crashed not breaking a bone or flower.
a list of cities crumbled under riots and distant gun-fire
yet the stone buildings sparkle. It is not only
the artificial lakes in the parks . . .   perhaps . . . . . .
but various illusions of belonging fall with equal noise and
    regularity

how could they know, the office girls as well
'fancy falling for him . . .'   and inherit a sickness
such legs fat and voluptuous . . .   smiling to himself
the length of train journeys

the whole landscape of surburban railway tracks,
passive canals and coloured oil-refineries.
it could be worse –

at intervals messages got through
the senate was deserted all that summer
black unmarked airplanes would suddenly appear
and then leave the sky surprised at its quiet
'couldn't you bear my tongue in your mouth?'

skin so smooth in the golden half-light
I work through nervousness to a poor but
convincing appearance of bravery and independence

mexico crossed by railways. aztec ruins
finally demolished and used for spanning one more ravine
in a chain of mountain tunnels and viaducts
and not one tear to span her grief
to lick him in the final mad-house hysteria
of armour falling off, rivets flying in all directions like fire-
    crackers,
and the limp joy of the great break-down
which answers so many questions.
a series of lovers – but could you? –
all leading through the same door after the first hours
of confused ecstasies.
the dream woman who eats her lover.
would suffocation be an exaggeration of what really happens?;
the man who forgets, leaving the shop
without his parcels, but meaning no harm.
'it's all a question of possession,
jealousy and . . . . . . ' the ability to torment,
the subtle bullying of night long talkings.
what artificial fruits can compare with this

and the wrecked potting-sheds that lie open
throughout the land?   gorging their misery
and that of others . . . geranium flowers hacked off the plants
by gentlemen's canes and now limp on the gravel
paths wandering through empty lawns and shrubberies
afternoon bickerings on a quiet park bench while
families take tea at a convenient cafe, so nicely situated.

engines and greased axles clattering through the shunting-yards.
fluttering parasols running for cover
under the nearby elms as the first heavy sweet raindrops
lick the girls forehead. the slightly hysterical
conversations crowded beneath the leaking branches
waiting for the july thunder to pass. the damp heat
and discomfort of clothes. a tongue passing the length
of her clitoris . . . . . . and back again . . . . . .
erections in the musty pavilion which should lead to a lake
but doesn't. the resin scent and dry throat in the pine wood
across the meadows.
                        'surely you remember?'
but so long ago.

strawberries lining her lake in the dark woods
an old picture slowly fading on the wall
as if a flower too could change her face
as a dusk cloaks our loneliness

Plato Was Right Though . . .

Part 1.

The empty house – the empty country – the empty sky.
Reverse it to A – B – C.

A: The large house
filled with many people – servants & guests –
it is now a country mansion.
It is white & has extensive grounds & woods.
There are many people.
They hunt & shoot. They laugh & talk.
In the evenings they play games.
It is all like a picture-book
that teaches vocabulary to foreigners –
each different object in the picture is numbered,
 & below are the lists of words that correspond
to the many numbers. So – 12 is table;
5: vase; 16: father . . . . . . & so on.

B: The full country.
The map blocked out with the red of cities
– that's the agreed colour in the atlas key.
This continues into the 3rd dimension with
'concrete & neon' parodying themselves.
Countries, armies, 'The People' struggling with
'The People'. The borders on the map look
so pretty, with dotted lines in bright coloured inks
– all yellows & reds – dot dot dot – & in practice
nothing more glorious than a stretch of
ill-kept road with a line of battered poplars
one side & strands of barbed wire on the other.
The bad spy story continues. . . . The plot is **very obvious**
 & stupid, even if it *is* all true.
No one could look at this & take it seriously.
And it wasn't just that the generals & borders
were ridiculous, but that the whole situation,
– including the very existence of the cities –
was wholly laughable.
The atlas became the one truely funny book,

& it did not escape our notice that what was portrayed
should be regarded in the same light.
To be totally 'negative' in believing the
countries as they were (& the cities) were
painfully absurd & grotesque seemed
perhaps the saner & more realistic.
It was a very pompous speech. . . . . . .

C: The sky was crowded with airplanes of all colours --
a totally unreal picture with dozens of
happy red, blue, orange & green
airplanes filling the sky in a mechanical
rainbow. Each plane, painted entirely in its
colour with no other markings, flies through a series
of aerobatic stunts, diving & climbing,
rolling over & over, & 'looping the loop'.
This is happening in a clear blue summer sky –
there has been no trace of a cloud all day.

Part 2.

All the previous locations are now impossible.
There is only this confusion in which no one
knows exactly what is going on.
The planes or the hesitating crowd on the lawns,
the house party going its usual way, –
but this only in a vacuum.
Outside is total darkness
dominated by the sure knowledge of Death
that takes on an almost human persona
& vibrates like the engines of an ocean liner at night
that can be felt many miles away & yet never seen.
(Black, as you know, is the negation of colour
& strictly it is not even a colour,

while White is all colours.)
And white is the love & only light that can be seen
to really exist besides the blackness.
The White is the only sure & real force
in an otherwise brutal chaos, & the only
home when all else has been lost.
(This new 'simplicity' was, in fact, a blessing
 & advantage never before possessed, & that now
made the struggle easier & brought a sure belief
in the victory that before was confined to day-dreams.)

A lone parachutist drifting down through the blue. . . .
And even if he *is* shot dead in his harness
by the border guards, who really cares?
He has the same chances as anyone else.
'When you're facing death or junk, you're always on your own,
 & that's exactly how it is,' he said. It became daily
more obvious that such clichéd truisms were only too true.

It is not a question of doubts or a lack of faith
in the forces of Good . . . . . . but from this black & white
landscape, what is it that will finally be launched?
There is an obvious & reasonable impatience
at the slowness of the expedition to set out &,
at least, attempt an exploration . . . . .   an examination
of what had happened in the past & what
could come out of the Interior afterwards.

Part 3.

The fact that there should be this co-existence
of opposites. . . . .   A desert, a barren plain, or,
to reduce this to its basic elements, a complete emptiness &
    darkness,

– faced by a crowded world of absurd objects
 & events, & a tangled 'confusion'; & this portrayed
quite clearly in a desperate heaping-up of words
 & pictures. The brightly coloured airplanes flying low
 & at great speed over the countryside & approaching the towns
brought a wave of cold fear upon all who saw them,
that the jollity of the planes' appearance at first denied.

It was this fact, above all, that was finally realized –
 & no matter how painful the realization, it had to be accepted
that what had gone on too long was due entirely
to a mental laziness that could live with this 'co-existence'.
There was no expedition to be expected or any news
of it to be eagerly awaited. If anything
was to be found or gained it would only come through
a 'personal action'.

                              'All the necessary equipment was there.
I only had to dress & begin.
And it was not a matter of fierce lions from the story-book,
or navigating my sampan through a wild & thundering gorge
only to have to fight 300 Chinese rebels the other side
single-handed with only a revolver & my walking stick.
The fun of these jaunts was a thing of the past.
What it meant now was to live like anyone else
– getting up in the morning, washing, eating meals, ...'

The convalescence, though once necessary,
was now over. All the wounds had healed &
the neat white scars could only be mementos.
This left no real excuses or causes for further delay.
'And the one simple & basic fact that love
had become a supreme power that radiated from me
was now the key to everything. And no matter how much
time would be needed, the struggle to deal with this
 & other pressures was there & only waited to be

used. Like the quiet in the ship's engine-room,
this inactivity seemed wrong.'

For some reason the word 'LOVE' does not suggest
a strength, or grace, only a mild ineffectuality.
Yet beyond the romantic charades & the gaudy neon letters
outside the theatre —   when the Real, &
the True essence is gained (or found), it's only this
love that creates a joy & happiness able to finally
dismiss a cruel haunting by Death, & meet the 'World'.
And what the words & poems attempt degenerates into this –
a clumsy manifesto in which the words used
appear emptier than ever before & the atmosphere
more that of an intense but bad Sunday School.
——————————————— PLATO was right to banish
poets from the Republic. Once they try to go beyond the
colours & shapes, they only ever fail, miserably –
some more gracefully than others.

Love in the Organ Loft

(*An Exeter Cathedral poem for Marian*)

The cathedral lay feeling rather damp among its trees
 & lawns, lichen covering its white stone walls
near the ground that is still wet from a rain shower.
It is April – of course. (Why should songs have all
the good lines? – like 'I love you', too.)

I'm beginning to wonder what I'm doing
 & what is going on? All I know is that it's now
very late at night, or early in the morning. . . .
You see, even this is disturbing & disordered.

T—CA—D

Is someone weeping in the street outside?
It sounds like a man. It is 3.30 a.m.
But when I go to the window, I can see no one.
I might have asked him in to cry in the warmth,
if he'd wanted. This isn't as stupid as it seems.
But everything on this (surface) level is so disjointed
that it can make even this possible act of kindness
appear to 'THEM' as 'foolishness' (if 'they' feel patronizing)
or 'absurdity' (if 'they' feel insecure that day).
(*A definition* of 'them'/'they': 'They' shampoo their cars on
Sundays, each holding a red plastic bucket.)

At 5.0 a.m. I am still watching over my love
– I love her more, so much more, than I've ever loved anyone,
even myself. In fact, this is a completely new
experience of *love*, like it is the first REAL time,
 & love for real.
                    'My eyes hurt now, but birds begin
to sing outside anticipating the dawn – though I can find
no connexion. Why should I? How absurd can I get
in this county town of the south-west province?
There appear to be no limits anywhere anymore.'
'His lips were sealed.' 'What is going on now?
You needn't doubt that I'll just wait –
"Faîtes vos jeux!" – until I get to the bottom of this.'

The cathedral & its own lush green & garden,
 & the comfortable & quietly rich church houses
with their private gardens that are set out
around the green – they are all peaceful & certain.
There is no question of escapism. (And it's about time
I woke up to this fact & appreciated the possible
sincerity of many such people & bodies.)

The birds masquerading as a 'dawn chorus'
have now become quite deafening with their twitterings
– I am sending for a shot-gun sales catalogue.

But what can this mean? – that I should
sit here all night watching over my love
 & at the same time I fix
more than double my usual intake
to feel without compassion my brain wince & flatten
under chemical blows –
cocaine memories now repeated, though on a less brutal scale.

I mean what is happening? – NOW! do you see
what I mean? – like does the cathedral nestle
in the sky's warm lap? OR does the sky
respectfully arch over the cathedral's gothic
towers & roof, flying buttresses & pinnacles?
This parable can be used for most things – think of a river . . .

The belief that ignorance is usually cloaked
in pompous wordiness seems well proven
by everything put down so far. And, in fact,
anyone feeling the need to relieve his by now strong
resentment of me will be, when possible,
met in all humility. I accept my guilt
 & am not surprised at these numerous 'accidents'
that seem to follow my progress through this city,
like falling slates & flower pots,
even a decanter of some form of alcohol
mysteriously dropped from a 2nd floor window.

But please, when you all feel relieved,
will someone tell me how it is I am
so blessed at last with a real love,
 – & this like I've never seen possessed by anyone?
But also . . . . . . & yet . . . . . .

And yet I know I need no explanations
&, least of all, justifications. The fact that the woman
I love with such continual & intense joy
& find what was before always transitory
an eternal & unshakeable happiness. All this
is this is this is this. . . . .   I'm so happy;
& now as she turns in her sleep,
her face's beauty fills me with a tenderness
& adoration that surprises even me, & fills my eyes with happy
   tears.

It's 6.00, & with the morning light
it seems my guard is over. No one comes
to relieve me – I couldn't stand rivals.
But why is the morbid masochism
of lines 48 to 50 still around? – Has it
no sense of decorum? All I want is to be able to
love as I'm loved & make my love happy.
Nobody here wants jack-boots,
or sleek viscious cars, or sleek viscious lovers,
or cocktail cabinets that play 'Jingle Bells'
everytime you open the doors – 'Oh boy!!'
All we want is ourselves – & that *is* really great.

But, please – if anyone has any answers
to the little problem of diet, do tell me.
I must go to bed now, but messages
can always be safely left here. Goodnight.
Good morning.
            The cathedral is so pretty
here, especially in spring – so do visit.

Michael Hastings

The Middle Classes Have no Hero

The middle classes have no hero, who
Must be their hero? I must. When I rode
Down express missive by train from Derby,
To an aunt who to stay with for ever
In Herne Bay at war – the barrels of sound
Thrust stutters of steel into the night jive –
I sat down a dull moment practising
With a toddler's fervor shallow dreams where
Soft sand and swept breakwaters filled my toes.
Uncle – I was told was slaying dragons.

I watched through the blind in blackout winks from
The pier spread slumped beneath laid sandbags,
Like a child's sled sunk into the darkness.
At night the planes' ack-ack and buzzsaw ceased;
The cajole of a comedian begged
The troops sit up and howl to the last dog.
Amongst this barrage of accord somewhere
Sang my Father in his three stripes and blue
About to die weeks away on Cologne.
He too, up the night sky dragged dragons, slayed.

What I most remember was their applause.
They replied! They joined in! The joke was at
Themselves to see their maim stupidities.
Too young to observe such rubbed nerve ends craved,
Had I known, the gay fornications
Of the unsmiling skull – their predator.

But I have learnt now with no war to frame
Their indulgences, up in the night sky
Now they are dead or dying of baldness,
Like they because I praise myself only
In the revolutions of the mirror –
I am the hero of the middle class
And will go down with jazz and moment
Like they, raized by the urn's compliment.

Spike Hawkins

Lights Seen

the rainbow hid in the car
    until the car stopped
and the man got out and threw
    away his entire family

Egg
(*for lee*)

I found a branch today
Some children had put it in a park
Your body the charred branch
I carried it over the river
I stood outside the ice palace
The branch waiting for the prams
I will put it in my bed away from all light
Though you are away from me in my bed
though light and hands rush you
there is tree flesh clanking as I lay
the forest and pick bark from my wet eyes
You giant bird are death my bed full of tree
It stands so like you black
In the morning when I am shaving
I tree will pick your vibrant mushrooms
you are my death, you are my death
Let you break the night in you from all my beds
Warm skin the glass cracked
You are here there is nothing to do any more

Hang your wigs in the sun
and pump up the dawn
Marsh gas leaking from a tree
Cycling through an avenue of green bottles
Tree you egypt of my legs

Shots from the park

The morning is realization of the dead Queen lying in your
   Garden surrounded by the floating retinue of those who wore
   out too many ships but set the seas on fire with their shouts
   of home and barlied bodies leaning up against Asian walls.
          with small boats and lotus
          forever floating
but never crushed by the drunken sailor
and never found in bed only in the bodies of
Gardeners whose gardens left when the rakes
split in the yard
and boiled out the moss from the well
and the leaves left on the front page
and the gardener turned deaf at the pain of the privets
whose roots filled the razors and hourglasses of those
who operated the machinery
The gardener is dead
flower pots breaking from his hands
to the wheelbarrows of his wounds
who is wheeled into all seasons
holding all hands and prams stuck
in the face of God
The milkman has discovered the gardener and the dead Queen
Empty garden has taken home orders
March off the faces have reappeared
from the direction of the Greenhouse

Early morning
cars stopping by the garden
sopped up the dead birds once more

Bleeg

(*for Robert Creeley*)

we have bought some food '
she has put it on the best table
we are not going to feed you
so go and stand outside in our
                    forest

West Eleven

(*for Roger Jones*)

rain after hot sun
filling my stetson with limp petals
My cycle clogged with mud
too tired I go home
leaving my lance stuck in his harmonica

Winter

You lying in my waterchute
sewing trees to snowdrifts
and the dogs staring at the halos
coming from the ground
the cattle drift up into the trees

Gloveparrot

I've been careless
I left my hat in the fire
The shape is there,
But when I touch it
I am burned
The japanese archer stares at me from the hill
I drive away, hatless

Raft

post by the side of me
swedish pine
no saw marks
but blushy
and slapped with tar
no good for a raft
and a quiet smoke

Excitement

smiles like cigarettes can be enjoyed
in bed
It depends on how you like your ornaments
tonight
with tickets for all the flights
                              I lie down to sleep
                              little with night

        eyes breaking into brittle animals

I sent a rich letter

Tasha I have won the goblet
and the free rosy plinth
Melissa sent a cable from
the Caribbean, it said 'Gratters'
The castle dance did swing
Were you tiddly, I mean stoned
Bunny Tucker is a stinker
Come and see my Goblet
I'm not washing since I
had the presentation
Man!

Shot Throughwithbrownlight

She fled from the carriage
In a flurry of sandwiches
That flew around the old man's head
Their springs broken
Like small fishes panting clank

Salad Days 1914

The flags that were
furling fell from the
half mast and started
patting one another in
the bushes
quite softly to begin with

Clean

the sitting wreath left
by the wellwisher
drove off in a car
after him

Tree Army Poem

alert ruin!
they shout
from the trees
. . . stupid bloody acorns

walk

walk
stupid animal!
silly animal!
stopping the traffic animal
RELAX!

Geoffrey Hazard

Song

A man a man
With pebbles for eyes
And mesh of steel for face
And a river in his mouth
And long head like a saint
And no clothes no clothes
   Only stars for trousers
     Newspapers for socks
     And dirt for shoes
     A man a man
     A great man.

Fairy-Tale

After the toys had gone
And the springs of the clock-work joys
Were destroyed, overwound,
The noise of the soldiers in the garrison
Drumming to the rhythm of a cry
Made the trees drop their leaves,
And blackbirds flew over the rivers of ice
Where snow lay on the banks,
And a crippled soldier was wrapped
In the snow by a snow-man smoking a pipe.
Drum, you toys in the garrison,
Drum your sorrow to the rhythm of a thousand cries,
And you, Jack-in-the-box,
Bite your red lips,
Roll your green eyes!

Piero Heliczer

England

1
then i realized we werent in england
but in a british movie

leaving behind two poppies
we went to england
heading for the sea it is hard
to write on a motorcycle
the airplane took off just like that
there was a pain of delight under my skull
i remembered cambridge and my first
bicycle ride me and bicycle
in some unknown suburb night and a ticket
to a e e cummings poetry reading in sanders theatre
i made it i was surprised at being
in an airplane
i had still enough marijuana in my lungs
to get high on inhaling cigarette by the time of landing

the customs people were nice
it would be easier to write this on the other side
of the paper but it is hard to think on a motorcycle
driving on the left as we must

the customs didn't know what questions to ask
me who would have thought however
that
i was interested in the fate of feathers

in effect carrying three of them across the border
one canadian one flamingo from a brussels zoo
and one spotted french one from a garbage heap

at the airport i thought
sir thomas wyatt was born here and said so
my motorcyclist was nonplussed
we are fifty miles from london
so the sheep say
there are no roadsigns because
the sheep are too woolly to see well
no one has taught them how to write either i shall
after the education in it i am receiving now
if i can write under these conditions a sheep can be taught how
   to write
i am interested in sheep i want to make that clear

you bloody english i yell to them
dont think they know what i am up to

we have just met another motorcyclist
what do you think he said i ask my motorcyclist
i dont know he replies
the motorcycle turns over
the sheep are amused but go on eating grass
the dead motorcycle snuggles up to a sheep
with an unweaned dead smile
the blue ball point pen lies rocking in the road
the back wheel careened over sunless river
of the english movie one father of american poetry
was already end over end over end over and
over
end

two bobbies came by
and as the two bodies had not as yet bought any english money
did not bury us

2

at maidstone we went into a bank an awesome place
i was very disappointed because i realized there would be no
   bathroom in the bank
which is what i had need of
at the bank they are using yesterdays rates
not in london
where they use todays

when we went to the bathroom in a public bar
we were enabled to leave our things unattended
because english people are so honest
i feel like writing every thing down
after i eat some thing i will read you some of the things i have
   written
maybe i should write that down

at maidstone my motorcyclist and i
walked out after paying
which we had already done
i had in my pocket
a twenty seven prize medals match box
also paid for
after we walk out we
plan to read some headlines
we would then like to be in london
we would like to be london
as i will think about how on their birthdays

they give bathrooms to cows in america
of a slightly better order than french humans use
which is why though americans are not thought to be
    conservative
there is no smell of cow dung in the fields
there is london my
motorcyclist will announce mysterious
city washed in fog

as the motorcycle left maidstone i waved to two english girls

i want to make clear that i like
english girls no one understands that
my motorcyclist says he does no one can
understand that i like english girls
i must make that clear i must write it down
so that no one understands it
as we entered county of london the road smelled like kief
gregory must have been here my australian motor cyclist said
his eyes were red like a kief smuggler
which he was
not green grey like it said in his australian passport
then we were going at thirty eight on the road side we passed
an extremely large picture of sir thomas wyatt
i brought it to the attention of my motorcyclist
i asked what speed we were making
thirty eight he replied
as i was writing we passed a big truck my motorcyclist
    announced
that said WE BUY FEATHERS

in the outskirts of london
a bobby put my motorcyclist on his honour

3
in a greenhouse retreat lavatory in regents park
i smoked my last american craven a
while i wondered at my motorcyclists white helmet
among the white tiles and urinals
we both thought this would be the best place to meet gregory
and allen in the meanwhile
my motorcyclist blew white smoke rings
with a cigarette he had lit with our last french match
but since we were driving on the left
we were really leaving london as we approached it
so we never got there
we decided it was
the end of the trip
our weights at the end of the trip were
for my motorcyclist eleven stone two pounds and
nine stone four and a half for me and nine three and a half
    without the record of the trip
we took our weights in the white lavatory
on green scale which cost a penny
the record weighed one pound but toilets we found only cost
    one penny

explicit england

Pete Hoida

vision of Portobello Road

There's a 1s. 6d. cinema,
a shop called Kaddish,
even smells of ginsbergs casbah
and garbage pails.
Tall corrugated tin bins,
lids shields against stolen railing
thrown by hole in trouser boy.
Screaming tricycles and melons,
lettuces and ripe negroes,
stripe shirt,
and others proud walking.
Its gay and sad and rich enough!

Did you ever see those Persil clouds

did you ever see those persil clouds
sailing up the madonna blue sky
no thoughts streaked across your mind
no places to go in dreams of orange and purple
no prissy strangers to stick outcrops of rock
in your gentle landscapes
no characters
like the orange butterflies settling on the blue plants
into the distant photograph
no position to prosidy the landscape of
stone flowers and sea
no neon eternity camp in your minds eye

no window for thoughts to streak
across the landscape, mother
your equations kindle
no doubt in my mind

Anselm Hollo

Message from the Border

A messenger,
  bald, his skin burnt onto his bones, he appears on the
    skyrim
  walking, not slowly nor fast, just walking: his bones move,
  his toe-joints grip the ground: he has been on his way,
  he will soon arrive,

We see him approach,
  we will see him arrive, we are his arrival: we will see
  how he opens his mouth, we will say: no! first – drink
    this!
  we will see how the water runs down into this sun-
    crumpled hide,
  filling out a few wrinkles,

And he will open his mouth
  and deliver the message: what will he say?

He will say what the one before him said,
  and the one before that one – he will tell us! The dancers! –
  the dancers – they – are surrounded! by the burning –

So simple it hurts . . . and always the same.
What else could it be?
What else could the messenger say
  these days? The dancers, in the midst of the burning . . .
    this

is the messenger's voice, the sound of his horn, abandoned
for lightness, and speed, now it lies on the sand
cracked by the heat, blackened – soon charred
by the black
heat

A warrant is out for
the arrest of Henry Miller
(*2 November 1962*)

GET THAT MAN!
    what rooftop
chases!   Zig-
       zag sprints in alleys
smelling of garlic
 & good fucks
      get that man!
      he's alive . . .
skittering
    down fire escapes,
the women watching
      with big startled tits
    rock-drill roar
    & torches flash
    down into fall-
      out shelters –
But all the while he sits on a mountaintop
 & smiles at sparrows hatching

at the foot of the ladder to man's heaven
 & says,   Yes   now
they're chasing
everybody.

requiem for a princess
Marilyn

Come & see the sleeping beauty wake !
the rocket cavalry charged her
womb-caves; write your name to pulse
forever on these purple walls.
Be voltage, one out of 500 million
charging her making her

jump & smile   .   jump & smile

till the lines harden & in the seething
mirrors she saw, Death.

*

> She made him a bed
> Drownd in a sack
> Shot in the back
> He sat on her head

Paper-tits tommyguns boys
mouthing 'love' with gunmetal eyes
– plaster the murderous walls
in Berlin anywhere in the world with her
glossy & naked awaiting
rape. There is no
love in it, it is the same
falsity. Stop
stop fucking yourself
dead things with dead things

*

Yet she whom they broke
bottles in trampled
across blew up
and out of her mind

is now with the other
who is oviform dark &
seldom shows her eyes

whose crime it was not
whose crime it is not

hear she is singing
to her by the river the black
waters O my
daughter:

*

Ballooning you rose
sea-born, froth & white softness
into our eyes our mouths
(by claws! you had fallen
into, on the dry
land) now yours
are closed, and nothing
could ever come out of you.

The river the black waters
have you, let you go a-
way, back where
those who are liquid
 & no hardness go:
not, ever, dust. Sea
rose unborn again,

blind breasts will open
in the deep and be
two flowers without name:
awaiting no one.

Song of the Tusk

The elephant
    bogged down
thousands
    of years ago

the fragmentary tusk
    now in a glass case

no no these are untrue statements
it is I
    who am in the glass case
        counting
            the stubs of museum tickets

it is the elephant
    who walks the downs
        who laughs at the sea
    growling

there is no such thing
    as thousands of years
I drop a stone on your head
    from the elephant's back
show me
    show me the thousands of years

I walk through the water
   throwing stones at the women on the beach
      the honeymoon women
         their eyes far apart

frightened
   they close the glass case
      over themselves and their lovers
         for thousands of years

well it has been a pleasure england

Well it has been a great old
party the first one said starting
on down the stairs a
great gettogether the second
one joining in all the others
pushing out into the stair-
case following them
on down talking and
singing and laughing like
mad supporting each
other stopping to pick up
this and that on the way
down the stairs a great
great long party winding on
down a merry old dragon of
Chinamen retelling itself
what jokes writing them
down on the walls for those
who came after stumbling
and hopping on down so pleased

No one noticed they must've
been going on down for at
least a month and well
                          below
                                    street-
                                              level

the fiends

One
by one,
caught out
in their secret gardens:

        sun in his head
leaning against a
Notting Hill lamp-post O hate
to see it go down
that dark cell drain
        hiding it in the TV set
neighbours told them,
'he never turned *it* on'
        or Camden Town basement
sounds laughter & smoke, *eheu
fugaces* O evil fruit
        pushing a pound of it
through Golders Green
a baby carriage, 2 babies on top
surprised at bobbies
groping around their damp bottoms
O drug fiends.
        Or on the way home on the Circle Line
6 packets of good Ghanaian
fell out his umbrella,

more in the bowler
O noeud de vipères
      & one with her lover man on her mind
          green seeds & leaves
     in her hair O vicious
Cannabis . . .

hello

The phone rings
     I lift the receiver
I say Hello to some utter stranger

he says Hello I am I
      he told me to phone you whenever I get here
& so I did I did get here I'm phoning you now
     this is a phone &
               I'm talking

& i heard a man, telling the sky

I have spoken kindly
without causing offence I have spoken kindly, politely
to customs officials wanting to know
the reasons for large amounts of peppermint tea in my pockets
kindly, a soft-spoken man
to policemen lifting me out of the rain & into the shelter
of well-built cells
to presidents, ministers, headwaiters & whores
all wanting to sell me what I never asked for
I have replied with a smile & a warm handshake
& a cheerful nod in passing

Nobody can even remember seeing me
except from the back, a peaceful Chirico puppet
receding into the calm perspectives of the city
pushing a red wheelbarrow full of plastic explosives
crossing borders unnoticed
in the guise of a walking egg
without causing offence
to rich & poor alike I have hummed lullabies

Tactfully I have given away bombs to rebels without private
    means
 & unobtrusively presented Alliance Commanders
with the latest in opiates & relevant literature
Walked out at dawn
my hands full of apples & candy for the haggard firing squad
apologizing for getting them out of bed at this early hour
Caved in at night
whispering words of admiration for the ingenuity
of my interrogators
Yes I have spoken so softly & smiled so much
my face has fallen away
This has encouraged me in my endeavours to be affable

I knew I was doing the right thing all along
My smile has increased in intensity
My eyes are fathomless caverns of admiration
 & flowers sprout
from my upturned nostrils of bone

Four Stills from *The Poet* (a film)
(*for Tom Raworth*)

The poet, drunk, is seen
composing a poem to the revolutionaries
of the world.

It is to be a long poem.

While working on p. 9 he realizes
that he is stone cold sober:
he stops, goes back,
reads what he has written
starts crossing out words –
lines – sections –
whole pages.

One line remains,
on page five. It says:

the heroes, their mouths full of

It is not
a very good line. Maybe
he only forgot to cross it out.
We cannot
ask him.
He has fallen asleep.

*

The poet,
asleep,
addresses his friends

You, my brethren
      in the dream:
remember the time of night
      we have agreed
to light our pipes of peace

Remember our pact
      be gently mad children
at the appointed hour
      paint the blue sign
on your foreheads

Knowing each other's rooms
      we can then be together
remember
      no one must know
our vow not to grow
      up in their world

*

In the morning,
the poet looks out
and sees a quiet residential neighbourhood

Look at it long enough
                        and it won't go away
talk to it long enough
                        and it will yawn
scream at it long enough
                        and it will dawn
upon you that Rome
                  was not overthrown
                              in a day

*

He returns
            to bed:
there is,
                possibly,
someone
            there.

Pomology

An apple a day
is 365 apples.
A poem a day
is 365 poems.
Most years.
Any doctor will tell you
it is easier to eat an apple
than to make a poem.
It is also easier
to eat a poem
than to make an apple
but only
just. But here
is what you do
to keep the doctor
out of it: publish a poem
on your appletree.
Have an apple
in your next book.

& How It Goes

Zoo-day, today
with the 2 young

'What animal
       did you like best?'
'That man'

She's three, more perfect
       than any future
              I or any man
              will lead her to

but now, to the gates
       & wait for the boat
              by the Regent's Canal

we stand in a queue
all tired, speechless

a line from Villon
       sings into my mind:
'Paradis paint . . .'
       'A painted paradise
where there are harps & lutes'

yes & no children
but who say such pretty things
       for me to inscribe
              in one of my notebooks
with the many blank pages
       marking the days
              I feel as forsaken as
                     balding François

T—CA—E

who also found
in himself
          the need to adore

     as different as my stance is
     here, in a queue of mums & dads
          down the green slope
               to the canal

– when he wrote to the Virgin
     hypocrite, setting his words
          to the forgotten quavers
of his mother's voice

     le bon Dieu
          knows where he'd left her

at least
          I'm holding her hand
     she's here, my daughter
     he is here
               'my son

the lives of the poets
     even the greatest, are dull
          & serve as warnings'

to say this, suddenly
     here, in the queue
          would no doubt be brave

he's half asleep,
clutching a plastic lion

'the thing is, they could not
    get out of themselves
        any better than these
who also wait
           for a boat

    – O that it were drunken,
        on what wild seas –
they didn't
    even try, just griped about it
        or made little idols
for brighter moments . . .'

The boat has arrived
    & there,
        the elephant's trumpet,
        farewell

Her weight on my knees
his head on my shoulder
        here
         we
         go

we, best-loved animals
    one,   two, three
        & as Illuminated
        as we'll ever be

Frances Horovitz

Bird

Leave the bright voices on the edge of the wood,
follow the bird quick
    arrow – messenger –
into the still shadow of the waiting trees.

  Light falls from leaf to leaf
  spattering gold is leaf is light
  and bird
  shadow swift
  falls – follows
       the air   – speeds
    in shafts of green
    vanishing invisible
    as echoing song ahead
  trails silence in the choir of trees.

Brown moss quiet underfoot;
Sunlight glitters in the empty glade.

moon

city bred
    I watch the moon
        through glass
distorted beyond vagary
    she rides
        the accuser
swinging tides
like recalcitrant skirts

her solitude breeds memory
heaves it to birth
mocks the still-born

moon, I remember –
your light a scalpel thrust
from a mouth of white bone

even through glass
I mirror your loneliness
walking in warm rooms

– sometimes I wish you
        no more than a thumbprint
on the edge of the sky

love poem

your total absence
rehearsal of my death

in this game
there is no substitute
all symbol gone
the knife flicks home
for real –

*

your silence
    spreads like water
        in an empty room

limp flowers
    in cellophane
        your gift
their scent rises
    a thin column
        leaning towards me

black trees
    barricade the sky
each morning
    we are ambushed
        by birds

your skull echoes

an inexhaustible fountain
        of sound

Michael Horovitz

Look Ahead

Our toes are ahead of us – they have grown out of us

Our nails are ahead of our toes – they keep changing colour

Our hammers are ahead of our nails – they strike like dockers

Our sickles are ahead of our hammers – shape of our hammer
    toes –

Our motors are head of our cinemas – our films are
        because we don't use gibbs
        state and church fight   tooth and nail
        whilst producers forge ahead of viewers

Our televisions are ahead of our patrons
        all is peddled

Our cycles are ahead of our tricycles and our trickles are
        our fashionable works of art
        trickled   by cyclists   on paint

Our best cyclists are our worst painters and

Our best painters are worse than our worst cyclists

Our worst cyclists are ahead of all our painters
        put together – save the painters become cyclists
        and that's what they've done –

every day more painters are taking up cycling
and daily they are discovered
biking up the strand
sponsored they swerve through swirls of paint
dribble ahead of trolleys trams trombones
start brushing their feet with gibbs
that cinemas accommodate motor cars at last

Our pedestrian toes hammer furiously on motorcycles
    but the hammers are sliced by sickles
    stuck hard by

Our frames our nails catch up with our toes till at last
    we're in
    we find our – teeth
    fully grown

    footballers   –

Thatched

I went to empty some ash out   the window
    still haven't brusht the cobwebs from   hair

City slicker mean wiles prowls
    melbasoft on peachskin suede

Free as air   the blind man stood
    on the road   and cried

Football hurtles from the park enclosure
    turtle shell glimmer

Red slips sail every washing day
    red wails in the sunset

A white feather lifts
    rams horn bellows   to the sky

'Ucelli in Testa'

Life is a disgusting riddle, but we can ask harder ones, was the Dadaist
attitude. To many intelligent men at this time, suicide seemed to be
the one remaining solution to the problem of living, and Dada was a
spectacular form of suicide, a manifestation of almost lunatic despair.
David Gascoyne, *A Short History of Surrealism.*

to have birds in the head is
    to be a little mad they say

so many same different things
    as   suicide is the only remaining

solution to the problem of life or
    suicide   is the only remaining problem

of life worth bothering about   when
    his car crashed into the tree the philosopher

was left with only death and its problems
    some people do things   others think about

doing them or no (things   machinedriven truisms
    about   in a) mad world what is sanity   for

drivers : THIS IS IT   for the religious
    there is a world   to come

and some   there is no words
    have birds   in the head

ParadiCe

The sky pink again where went
the ground all one
Aaaah the fierce energy in those motorcycles
A milk-bottle flute
Walk now
the warm green sun
Perspectives
all doors opened   Quietly
voices trickle through
little feet through
the floor   Fingers
sift silt from clay
between the tiles
feeding worms
the eavebirds playthings
Domestic ranges wilde –
I see what I never have seen

Yet   know it will go from me
I want too much
to grasp and hold the key
turn over to others as if
from me   reaching out
to clasp to know
the beams of love
dissolve in my hand
dun the paremeters of land
The radiance turns to hail
I pace a crazy pavement joyless
   above is
         atomized
      sections of the

world   gone grey
brought down
Trapped in my image
Mine owne –

Halls of anguish

Mirrors of trembling

Everything Looks So Good in the Window

sleep after the first
awakening is never the same

the grass drank deep in the night
rust thickens, mists descend
in the long night

no good that
trying to catch up on dreams
straining the eyes shut
fighting the dayglow – no, up

to swerve through the dawn clearings
unlock the throat of early birds
into street games, the greens and

the gross   net   traps –

Danger – Men at Work

Collages of humanity we may be
maimed by governments elect

for arms arms arms
but one thing's for sure –

ARMY   SURPLUS

– as announced by West End stores
ever since the last three wars

LAST THREE DAYS – !
EVERYTHING   *MUST*   GO!

– NEWS OF THE WORLD?
Closed for Mars –
'ALL LIFE IS HUMAN THERE'
(The rats race like people –

Making it
corrodes
like hard-
coloured rock
through & through
you can eat
rock
but the system
eats
you –

Dangermen at work
– charging the earth

The price remains long after
the value is forgotten –

'eat well – *eat Walls*!'
– and shit bricks –

if you take in every –
thing they say
You can't help falling –

God's in His Heaven
    Creating Earth
When He gets down here
        He's going to raise   Hell –

Soho Awakening

mind's eye opens afresh
from dreamgleam trance

in a pool of petrol
all tones dance

crescent   city   moon
incandescent   through vapours
cuts   back to the arc
of historic   time

sun's spectrum swells
in park enclaves
rainbows plash
off ducks back waters

yea like a sainted medieval spirit
winding fresh flowers
through the black death
dawn   hits   town

piercing skylight and airshaft
through these salvage dumped streets
and bird-brimming squares

even glances down
the underground

'Spring Welcomes You to London'

 – the poster sings and a merry
engine washes the Soho streets
No dragons no nets it's good
to be up and about – till
This man 7 a.m. Sunday sunshine
cowering on the Astoria steps
grabs three pigeons★ deaf
to their agitated cooing stashed
in his plush red shooting-brake
– What, I shout before he can slam the doors
What are you taking the pigeons away?
– Whadd'ya mean what am I taking the pigeons away?
What's it look like I'm doin'?   – But why?
They've as much right as you to roam the city
– and they're pretty –   Pretty ? ?
That's what you think isit ya gett –
Take a good look: they Shit allover the place
No hygiene . . . What we call
Trafalgar Square's buried under their droppins –
They use the roads as airways
An' dive under the cars –
And the more on'em there are
The more they reproduce their 'orrible selves
– There's bye-laws bein' passed. . .   And in chimes
a hatchet-faced policeman loomed abreast:
They pick the silver tops offof milkbottles
for beatniks to drain an' smash –
Shit, I say to myself, What   – but behind our backs
a tiny wizened cleaningwoman's pissing herself
with laughter – the birds flapped up the basket-lid

★Pigeons = 🐧 🐧 🐧

and out after breadcrumbs she's sprinkled
there on the open street they dodge the traffic
a busy crooning throng of doves pigeons robins sparrows –
Multinous fowl breakfasting at her behest then
shimmering up the treetop green of Golden Square
delivered by wings from civic petty fogs
and the lurking scraowlcats to boot –

Soliloquy in the Forest

                            . . . Hard pressed between the
leaves of the soul's black book, a poor suffering poet conjures the Muse
to relinquish her patronage:

                    I'm well-dressed Robin
                              the Hoodest
          redbreast –
                              a bit   – under the crest
        'cos I'm plagued all night
            by an amorous pest
    who comes on   with a raging unquenchable quest
                              even unto my very nest
              with intent to dishonourably unzip
                    my sleep skin vest

                    It's obvious
                              I'll get no rest
          until I prevail upon that   blithering
                              babbling   bluetitted
      moon-madding museumpiece of a   – Muse
            & uninvited guest
    to renounce her foolish dream   of my pillarbox chest
                              pressed

                    upon hers (for I am betrothed
                              to an ex-
                                   tremely well made
                                             Marionbird –
                         the best!)

                         'List, twitmus –
                                   'tis no jest:
              this union's blessed
                              by all that's not retrogressed
         & cessed.   Move West, distressed
              fowl, or get messed about
in any direction you like   lest – in your zest
                                   to attest
              your conviction we'd make bosom pals
                    thou forgetst

                    I could have you   –   arrested
                                        for molesting
         by the Sherriff   of Notting-Hill-Gate –

Man-to-Man Blues

It takes a man to make a woman, takes a woman to make
   him a man
Yea – if a man makes a woman, it's her who makes him a man
But *I'll* make it on *my own* – I will – I know, I can –

Any man? *Every*man? – No man, M. E. – *me*!
Aah brave man rave man – A whambam thank*you* wee
– Absurd to be a bird – but it's crazy to be free.

We're all washed up, you left me high & dry
You made me cry – but now I can fly real high
Yes – wanted to die but now I'm flying high –

You can – do what you please, go snip your hollyhocks
Wou'n'like to be in my shoes – well, you needn't wash my socks
But if you think you've *had* the blues, just dig *me* on the box –

'Hey man-beau . . . Go man – Melt me 'til I'm gone
He - man you're on the ball – so *han*'some – shee, some man!
Mister Sandman please   send me – a life span jazzman-man . . .

'I'm in heaven – wow, how high the man
Can't help loving that man O man divine –'   then
Tune you OUT dead drunk from that groove-juice of mine.

Trust that woman   make monkey out of you –
Kick that man habit man, she'll say & mean it true
Then turn you off & whip you into glue –

  with her Manday at 8, don't be late,
  & her Man, you're *too much* man
  till her passions abate & switch to hate
  & you're there just to carry the can –

  with her *Come*-ON, here boy –
  thump me out your innings;
  Hit it hard – give me *all* your joy –
  man, & *I'll* chalk up the winnings –

  with her Hey man   straw man
  What   are   you   trying   to say man –
  she'll drive you round the bend
  & ride you straight back again:

  she makes you feel like Shelley man
  & the minute you show you know it
  she'll put you down as an *Also* man
  – bet your life on some other poet

Take her man   loverman – but
better rise above her man
or What a Gas Man turns to grey man –
Hang her up – Or pay man –

Pick her up, and shake it
– cut out sharp, & break it –
Tell her – Man a man, go 'way a man
– come again a man – an*other* man!

> The sky's the limit
> you float – you flow
> you're happy to come
> you happen to go –

> If you care
> you don't know
> – You know?
> You don't tell

> – Think you're in
> Heaven?
> Well – you'll soon be
> in H
>   E
>   L
>   L –

Comes the time when you're *un*stoned – discover to your cost
Yea – you're stone cold sober and find out what you've lost –
That woman who loved you, the one that you need the most:

You've done your nut, you've flipped – you're *gone* – berserk –!
Gone all to phut – now that ON-moon light is dark:
You plan your plan, but how can you make it work?

Your day is done
 & what *do* you know –
You come down with the sun
and you've GOT to go –

the tabula rasa
of the way out mind
visions knock you out
– and leave you   kind

You'll come to go & go to come
to kick over all the traces
Then meet, and break – to meet again
 & mend at the broken places –

Before they bury you deep in no man's land
'fore you go for ever – make out, make it   grand
Man, meet your maker, and shake her by the hand

        – Takes a good woman to make a man a man
        Wake up brother – find her
        And love her   as true   as you can.

Memo

(from Wm Blake
to sundry   psychedelinquent   whizz kids
assuming   his name   in vain):

Stop bleating
about the bush
little lambs

Get wean'd
Or get   stufft

(in some body
else's   pram --

World's End – Happening –

. . . Dancing   upstaires
'thinking' about   'my' penguin
– nearly trod
                    on   – the cats !

Throw Away Your Keys for Bodies Contain
   no Locks they Understand –

praliné pramsqueaks sweetness of lazy afternoonstreats
paté   the far grass calls and each call is answered
rite courteously   the waterfalls never cease
fumbling into foam till   finally fieforfumfreed for fun
frolicy fish flicker childeyed   several candles
suddenly speak from the forest   black birds
gather round them singing the rivers inside clouds
whose burst winds shake out   fruit
ful artuilery of leafwhispers
                          lights a clearing
in each fragrant heart   unfolding   to this day's   sun

Frances

Your eyes are islands
Lord – cast my soul
Ashore – Oh Beauty

Your body – even in sleep
All Paradise.   We are one
In love – two, knowing that
And three – apart

And four – by this grace
Of making, of facing
Each other, and our selves.

When I spring, from dream
To write – you stir
Murmuring – 'my long lost . . .'
Images – mosaic
Fragments – reassemble

The poem – land-locked yet
Complete – as Blake's vast
Vision – yet more real

Now time stands still

    As out of mine

    Deep into your
    Eyes I see

    That you are
    Life to me –

Libby Houston

The Tale of the Estuary & the Hedge

'Come,' said the small slimy
estuary, pleasantly, 'Come,'
to the hedge that guarded
the door of the low-lying meadow.

'Follow me along my easy course,'
smiled the mud, 'Oh,
your butter won't turn,
your daisies won't run,
I assure you, you won't be away for long.'

Doubtful, the hedge packed
its hawthorn blooms, sparrow nests
and ditchweeds neatly in a bundle
to follow, with a guilty look behind:
Had the Meadow noticed?

Hour on hour lazily
the little estuary
crept and curved:
the hedge trotting after.

The air became brighter,
new the birds that swam
or perched momentarily,
net-heaps ousting ploughs
and the estuary gaining in girth.

Now! Like an ambush,
round the corner, the land
Stops! The hedge is lost!

'It is The Sea – it is only
the sea,' smiles on the estuary,
'Don't be yellow-hearted, come,
follow, I'll be leading you.'

Mark Hyatt

Smoked

It goes through the body like a satellite
    because one wanted it that way
        holding back a mouthful of air
            trapped in the tears of doom.

Looking at the most beautiful thing in the universe
    known in the dictionary as a human;
        what is it in these eyes that burn?
        the knowledge of tragedy.

O let time spin around this mind right now
    & the liquids of these eyes be forever lissom
        because the substance of the mind feels like lead.

The same old blood runs on, in crime-philosophy
    digging the aged invisible kick
        to put one's-self on an electric grid
        & fray with years.

I hope the war in the apple-orchard ends soon
    for all the missiles I've are filled with love
        and they will drop like birds from the sky
            on the drawings of desire in this heart.

All Sunday Long

A knife
hits my back-bone
as a sparkling boy
puts wires
through my head.

Through.
A cold steel hammer
beats on my chest.

In the cracking up
of my body
my organs are being sorted
by master eyes;
as a shadow walks into life
and purple colours.

I move
cold as a fish in hell
shaking my body.

And again, the boy
combing my body
with an electric comb.

My eyes long to fall out.
My lungs are loose at the ends
as I am;   disappearing
I got into two pieces
or more;
pains of me; jumping
into stiff pains.

And madness is setting in;
    now I am crying
        and I don't exist
            but somewhere in my past –
            I must have felt a need for me.

Sh
Everyboy

The Clown stares at me
                as if I made him
    Two broken eyes
                Coal-black & Steel-cold
Sad He is
        by the cold air around him.

Moon-head
        think
            I've no answers
                only a mind pickled in blood.

Clown
    I see the War-Face
                    Hiding behind shadows
    I feel fire
                in burnt eyeballs
            smell gas
                    what a way to play
    I know you're trying to drug me
                into war.

Come Clown orbit through my head
                if my head is large enough?
                    I change in the Light
                              sweat & spin
        like black-ravens
                – caught in a cob-web
        or whip me with age
                But
                Accept through your own mind
                    I've no visions.
No-Lovers
        No-Bombs
                No-Air only me
                I am being filtered by choice.

        Why Narcosis when I am thinking?
                Its sleep upon knowledge.

answer don't move

I see artiliery friends evaporate
into lousy night trips,
they can't murder me
for fear.
Benches of cowards
calling:
pretty queer;
they know their own voices.
I fly my dreams
 & motorbike lovely sweet heaven
looking for my own dead.

We're coin pretty,
Lovewish,
Absolute devils on earth.

Treat me carefully
because I am bleeding truth
and that shit.

You want what I want, bastard.
Your after my life.
You twisted snot . . .
picking out the gold.
Your not silly but I am, somewhere.

Queer little things
I think you are only human joys
but of you of me:
Little coward hello,
Looking down the corridors.
Yes, I am coming
like water on a desert
to feed the hopeless
and the lost
but they are small in number.

I will drag your motionless life.
Across hell with me
into the dark fear called mind.

Eleemosynary

I spread the Latin wings, a Moth, dressed like
a hairless rat, heading for a grain of light,
exposed to your fear, a mere figure of sound,

the tax-gatherer to Judas, in a pilgrim's
fight around the asylum, its one phenomenon to
another, the virgin composing a language,
neither in paradise or the nutshell of knowledge.
Mark this well, my rare courage of leprosy is
not from the empire of defeat, but the blacksmith's
hours of leisure, I am out seeking to entice,
holy nice pride thats buried in the sands, no one
astonished, and enter friendly conversation,
saintly like, nearly killed by a debtor, am I
the damned tormentor? Out for the infernal
banquet, a feared king of darkness, fat on
fragments of huge committed mankind, violent with
my shadow, a countryside poverty, the desperately
fallen marriage of laughing-shock, with unmasked
documents about the rendezvous, freely lavishing
on a lady's honour, meanwhile the years go on, the
triumph of the spectators, flogs on sight.
The jugglers work below on small talent, in the
human legions, out to kill, me with my adventurous
deeds, there's no intermission on any vice, the
idleness of wealthy knowledge flies, teeming with
sad shepherds, beginning to end, chilled relaxation
with an emperor's heart, the victim of a curse, a
devil's stench, hitting the wall again and again,
flying this dangerous journey, erected by night, a
horrible tempest, this my imagination transforms down
the court, one day in the dead, another fashioned
by the custom of hell, of foretold future, without
the rank of a wizard, an angel in everlasting bliss
praised by punishment, this wicked necessity to journey
with my cloak and secret sight-seeing, past a
numberless count of heroes, forced by the fiends,
sometimes burnt by jealous heretics because of an

arena with its multitude of visions, their
utter ruin, others possessed nothing.
Now I am flying towards the experienced champion,
and I am stuck in the middle of a cob'web, soon the
beast will come down and suck my body, a sunbeam
will bring confusion, it must be the adversary, the
task of conquering must be choice, wrinkled and bent
she comes, this queen engages the gigantic circus
crowds to recognize the enemy, with promise and pledge
she comes forth, dragging her injections of new tortures,
its got to look like this, one passive and suffering
moods, the active, singing on the hour of conception,
making eyes at the subterranean Pluto of Liverpool,
intimate bonds fall like fortresses of opinion, its the
same practical joke played by every other saint, the
modern Babyloinian greed, thinking youth concealed a
treasure, but youth hold the very thing Solomon placed in
a vase, to avoid publicity of pop delusions, my killer is
a friend, unable to make any answer, its the on-lookers
that slash the mind, for death.

John James

Ah - Leu - Cha

edge of paulton,
                north somerset,
might be any other little place tonight,
 & any hedgerow
                    might be smudging
                                    the division
between any thistle-ruin'd field & sky
loosing clarity
                through misty trailing clouds
 & smoke
            from a couchfire
the gawky elms cottages
depressed left side
                        the rise
nearer
        the new unmetalled road
bricks blocks gravel mixer
clay smothering topsoil
where speculators
                    fumble the land
 & as fast as the pencil marks the page
these things blend to darkness so
the light which has been glowing
on a pole over by the sunken lane
sharpens to a star against
black foliage. But
the greatest illumination is
propelled from these horns,

this record, this ah–leu–cha now,
parker's horn that posits
making this view
                    tolerable

Bathampton Morrismen at the Rose & Crown

The glossy saloons slide up the rise.
The dancers, faces oblivious & grave,
block them –

white cloth vibrating
against dark green hedgerow, the tiny bells sound a
fraction of a second before a leg is seen to move –
the heavy flesh leaps – thick thighs bring the hard heels down –

HWAIGHH! – sticks clack on tarmac,
whap overhead.

When it comes, Renolds, with graceful nonchalant wrists
flicks his pair of handkerchiefs at a bass yell of thunder.
His soul flashes briefly in the white of an eyeball.

The solo dancer leaps,
straight & upright, chin hanging,
mouth of big broken teeth,
eyes rolling upwards in beatific idiocy,
looks into the interior of the heavens, the growling clouds
their innards exposed –
static explosions of rose & cream, Rose & Crown & roses still
    here

despite bombs in the 40's –
Jim leaning on his stick at the door
saw the limbs of trees
dislocate towards him –
a fast mass of air blasts atop the ridge,
goes clear over the roof of the house,
windows break in Timsbury
on the higher hill behind –

Renolds' sons dance too,
the smallest? – 8?
exactly following the five
men, advancing retreating,
stepping back up into the hedgebank
when pushed for space by his elders.

The saloons cannot get through.
Everybody ignores them –
they'll have to find their own gaps.

Strawberries & snails
sinking & rising
in my cidercup.

Roger Jones

'imagine me on the street'

imagine me on the street
handing out my pamphlets
this man comes up
and i say 'have one'
but he says 'have one of mine'
so we trade

i look at the paper he gives me

inspired by this free and
friendly exchange of
mutually irreconcilable ideas
i fall to thinking 'great!
that's democracy for you'
and when he is out of sight
i tear it up without reading it

Two Fables

1.

Once there was a cannon ball and
every time he felt himself whizzing
up the barrel he shouted 'FIRE!'

After a bit he became interested in
existentialism and took to shouting
'WHY NOT?'

2.

There was a little man who
stole an orange from a table

The house ran after him shouting
'That's my bicycle!'

Imperial War Museum

brown
horses flopped
sideways in the mud   /
khaki uniforms

four years of brown dying
fifty years ago
remembered now
in old
brown
photographs   /

David Kerrison

The Third Compassion

The entry into Hiroshima was in the bay
of the B-29, death called 'Mr B' with exquisite oriental charm.
Out of the morning sun crept the lonely bird,
the American Eagle, four props of glass turning
slow in the sunshine.

First came the light quick on the slope of the morning
sending dark faces in the dust, vain prayer;
arose with blood on their backs.
The city began the gentle ceremonies of death.

They watched the darkness come down
burning and touched with blood.
A child crawled out of the ruins trying to die.
Hair twisted in flames that was so straight and black,
not quite digested by the fat, glass bird,
thrown back like a fly, head wet with fire.

The sun shall rise and set no more.
The rising sun melted in the straight, red wind
which lifted pavements
and scattered lives like orange-peel.
The chosen ones, on the smoking blackened tree.

Silence after the moment of the bomb,
on the eyes of the children;
the communal suffering was silent.
The city silent on the sign of the two crossed sticks.

There were three compassions;
the one for the man was burnt,
the second, for his child, was lost in the ruins,
the third and last remains, just;
for his child's unborn, dying children.
And here stand the others, in the blank dreadful stare,
watching the faceless child who crawls before them,
who cannot gaze, who had no eyes,
who cannot lift his twisted hand,
who cannot sleep, who cannot die, who was not born.

Yellow Blues – on the murders in S. Africa

Shall we smooth away the stones of blood
that litter the streets of the quiet dead,
and whisper 'forgive'?
Shall we walk on the congealing blood and brick,
stamping a practical road
from the red clotted leaves,
saying 'forget'?

Either way, ten million Jews and Negroes
press on our murderers' strangled souls
and Christ is still cursing the monster he bore
on the crooked black cross
while the black-shirted cripples danced round.

And somewhere there is a glittering horn at work
singing a slow fine unhappy sound,
a yellow stream of thought and heart,
a bloody, nervous horn of glass,
as the sun leans on the egg-shell pyramids of death
built by the dying hordes,
the beloved, scornful, weeping children.

Forget the song.
Forget the fading horn.
Release them.
Loose the tears from the white blown eyes,
and see the croaking reed hang
in the dry red bowels of his broken throat.

Servia Hill — Leeds 2

Damplight season.
A million broken steps and streets.
And the music of Ornette Coleman.
Mooncry.
Kiss.
Love.
The footsteps of drunken God.
The curtains are streaked with the smiles of
lepers.
And the music of
this blasphemous life
startles
me.
Spiders fall with the dusty rain kissing my
blistered heart and stopping it
dead.
A broken abandoned rainbow lies on the ground.

Poetry

To strangle the wind is really something,
And trying to tell a little of love
is hard, with a throat full of sand to dissolve.

And the white birds are always high.

A broken button from a faded coat carries more than the devil
to bring the knee in your groin and blood in your mouth.

Sky spinning upside down within you;
brick and bone mingling to make the child with yellow hair
grow out of you, that will murder you.

And in the last sequence of evening when the stones
warm the roofs and the lights are dimmed to it
and your head is filled with it,
and your tongue feels it sitting,
you are quite outside of it and away from it,
sitting on blue empty rooftops fingering the moon.

Seymour King

Chance Shots

a silver knife and fork raised point to points part
and plunge into a meal of wreathes
a hat is raised slowly with solemnity
only to emit ascending underwater noises
a set piece of false teeth and a lit cigarette appear
on a black top board of a diving tower
a duck plops into a pastoral scene painted on a tumbler
to a train whistle puffing smoke
a red light clangs and everywhere crowds act out angers
separately and without a sound
cars all green roar across an imitation plastic ploughed field
an astonished mouth lets out a burst of pidgeons
nelson and churchill are rocked in battleship cradles
by mental nurses and nuclear disarmers lullabying welsh
accented
clad in soccer outfits and miners helmets
leaves fall upon a bible on a fifty foot pillar which opens
to cynical groans conducted by a peppered white verger
words float through a dull sky and a salesman in blue suit
gold hat and white tie advertises washable sounds beside
a demonstration outside a cinema foyer for dictatorship
of meaning on one infallible level a line of men smiling
fatuously look in on a circle of fierce looking women
attempting desperately to close their legs
a poet at a snooker table rips up the cloth with his cueshots
while the coloured balls hang about his head from the shade
and a pen writes itself on a pad by his drink and book he
coughs and a thermometer registers zero on a cracking plate

a newsflash on the radio IS IMAGINATION RETALIATION
opens
a trapdoor out of which fly an associated examiners league
clasping hands religiously and ring a ring a rosiely artists
tattoo self portraits on their wives backs lineing up their
brushes to a tape recorder offering worms to the future to
heavenly music as its reel unrolls into a tray of acid as a
skeleton puts on a coat of flesh and walks through the water
of a nightshore smirking knowingly up and back to an outside
judge and jury in phosphorescent benches sucking poison
sweets

A Clock Twice

at first sight the clock alone
drives light from its face
handless limitless flat ticking space
an hour or so later
an hour without length
on the slippery face of ephemeral love
in the fight of the smoke of a train of events
to find the open of a named arrival
in the signal of becoming something other than thought
on the pain of perhaps when there is no ought
the clock is white and points to the time
in a flash of plane through the shift of light
to its coat of paint on a coloured whim
to the sideboards unknown life for its stand
to the ring on its top for a hand
to the time for the end of a search of the single mind

AD Voice of 2000

we dont want you people to kill
we dont need you people to stamp out our will
our space heads are filled with nuclear thoughts
our trigger fingers are happy with flowers under newclear skies
we are warning you with flowers that cannot be bought
for more than the sun can smile
we give you the freedom to pass thru the stars of our eyes
if you promise to look for more in yr heart
than you pretend to know and dont see
but like to see to avoid the traffic of dangerous hopes
we shall spy in yr coffins you build nearer each day
we shall sing in yr toilets when you glare at the news
we shall pay for nothing but the price of living it free
for giving ourselves to our customers free
by speaking of all things carefully
by sharing our lives with yr bread and speech
we shall empty yr dustbins you call discretion
we invite you to join in the party
that has no policy or police
minuteness or madness of laws
that has no name or memory
that flies from heart to hand to mouth
that takes by laughing and gives emptyhanded
that holds you to living
the glories you can live by dreaming
– the organs of publicity are dead
– the heavens of our bodies are alive
when we greet the night we were born from
with the light we can dream thru by being ourselves
– yes! it is written in the tracts of our blood

we journey together – only our names are different
and our experiences for ever
make love last   last
yes last out to the moment we always live

Bernard Kops

The Sad Boys

The sad boys of the afternoon
are wandering through the town,
looking for some lonely girls
to lay their bodies down.

The sad boys sit around and croon
but never lose their frown;
no one comes and no one goes;
they watch the leaves twist down.

The sad boys of the afternoon
pull petals from the park,
then throw them at the dying sun
and stroll into the dark.

skyman

my god I'm dead –
the young man said

when he saw his battered head
petalled on the crimson sand

– oh mother come and meet me now
and take my hand –

his body like a fountain played
along the empty esplanade

a cococola sign winked on
and when the moon came he was gone

Shalom Bomb

I want a bomb, my own private bomb, my shalom bomb.
I'll test it in the morning, when my son awakes,
hot and stretching, smelling beautiful from sleep.
Boom! Boom!
Come my son dance naked in the room.
I'll test it on the landing and wake my neighbours,
the masons and the whores and the students who live down-
　　stairs.

Oh I must have a bomb and I'll throw open windows and
count down as I whizz around the living room,
on his bike, with him flying angels on my shoulder;
and my wife dancing in her dressing gown.
I want a happy family bomb, a do-it-yourself bomb,
I'll climb on the roof and ignite it there about noon.
My improved design will gong the world and we'll all eat lunch.

My pretty little bomb will play a daytime lullaby and
thank you bomb for now my son falls fast asleep.
My love come close, close the curtains, my lovely bomb,
my darling,
My naughty bomb. Burst around us, burst between us, burst
within us,
Light up the universe, then linger, linger
while the drone of the world recedes.

Shalom bomb

I want to explode the breasts of my wife.
And wake everyone,
to explode over playgrounds and parks, just as children
come from schools. I want a laughter bomb,
filled with sherbert fountains, licorice allsorts, chocolate
kisses, candy floss,
tinsel and streamers, balloons and fireworks, lucky bags,
bubbles and masks and false noses.
I want my bomb to sprinkle the earth with roses.
I want a one-man-band bomb. My own bomb.

My live long and die happy bomb.
My die peacefully of old age bomb,
in my own bed bomb.
My Om Mane Padme Aum Bomb, My Tiddly Om
Pom Bomb.
My goodnight bomb, my sleeptight bomb,
My see you in the morning bomb.
I want my bomb, my own private bomb, my Shalom bomb.

Whatever Happened to Isaac Babel?

Whatever happened to Isaac Babel?
And if it comes to that –
whatever happened to those old men of Hackney
who sat around a wireless, weeping tears of pride
at weather forecasts from Radio Moscow?

Whatever happened to us? The Lovers of Peace?
And to our proud banners?
Whatever happened to our son?
And to that Picasso dove of Peace
we brought him back from Budapest?

Whatever happened to that little man
who tried to leap above himself?
He had a fire in his eyes;
a certain beauty in his eyes.
Or maybe that was merely poverty.

Whatever happened to Vladimir
Mayakovsky? Sergei Esenin? And Leon Trotsky?
Between the Instant Quaker and the Colour Supplement
we are apt to find no time to talk of them.

But then, we are apt to find no time to talk.

Now it is day,
and rather late in the day.
Whatever happened to us?

We are the worm contractors;
lusty youths of fire have become tweeded teachers,
with a swish Hi-fi that was bought for cash
and a smashing collecting of Protest Songs.

Oh ye dreamers of peace!
Dreamers of bright red dawn!
Whatever happened to that dream?
The dead are buried and the years
and forests of computers cover us.

We are crushed within the heart.
We are gone like prophet Leon
with ice-picks in our brain.

But there is no red stain.

We leave nothing behind
except volumes and volumes; such beautiful
volumes.
Unread but rather splendidly
displayed upon tasteful teak.

Oh ye sitters down for peace!
Only the pigeons protest
these days down Whitehall.
Oh Comrades of Slogan Square!
This is a windy Judas corner;
this is the fraught, frozen over winter park.

I smile and walk backward.
If you insist I am also part of this.
But through my clenched teeth
I somehow cannot stop myself chanting.

Whatever happened to Isaac Babel?
Whatever became of me?

I think often of Isaac Babel,
of his unsung death.
And as I walk away from you
I know that I am all full up.
I am all full up with people.
I have no vacancies.

Suicide at forty would be mere exhibitionism.

Besides, I have songs to sing.
Songs for myself;
songs to keep me warm;
songs to feed into mouths.
And I have one mouth in particular to kiss;
and eyes above that mouth from where I draw
my songs.
He was a funny little man, Isaac Babel.
And one would have thought him a nonentity,
had they not needed to dispose of him
so thoroughly in the dark.

Most people in this world are worthwhile;
therefore I can dispense with most of them.

You have to draw the line somewhere.

Yes, I think often of that little man
'with glasses on his nose and Autumn in his heart'.
Isaac Babel! Can you hear me?
I think often of your untelevised death.

Whatever happened to us
Returning from Whitehall
our banners smudged with rain,
our slogans running away?
Us waving, shaving, running after
our going youth and euphoria.
Hurtling through these fattening years
of hollow laughter.

And incidentally – who are we and
where are we?

So dreams die.
My dreams.
So can you blame me for building
barricades in West Hampstead?
Nice flat. Garden flat; unnumbered,
somewhere behind the Finchley Road.
With children laughing and children crying
and within me still one thread of longing.
And one wife calm and warm, belonging.

So – where was I?
Oh yes! Whatever happened to ——————?
What was his name?

Never mind, nothing really changes;
except children grow,
and we realize there is nowhere else to go.
There is only us now. Us alone.

And not forgetting that rather funny
little jewish cossack fellow
who at the moment slips the mind.
Not to worry, they're bound to know his name
in Better Books.

There is a certain joy in knowing;
but then again a certain peace and quiet in
half forgetting.

David Kozubei

Tragedian's Speech

Death, death, death, alas;
Death, death, death, alas;
Ooooooooooooooooooooooh
Woe, woe, woe, woe;
Death.

Poem

black words,
who torn –

and you
who woods
adorn

extent –

incredible the last,
amazing –

greet,
and the words
frothing
seek.

Herbert Lomas

The History of Conscience

Looking over
What are surely
National Health Spectacles

Fumbling papers
And wearing a toga
Surely some joke

That's what the
That's what the
Prosecution says.

'But I preferred
Reality, not fantasy.'

That's what the
Prosecution says

The prosecution
Says you preferred
The stand shared in common.

'That was reality!
I tried to be
I tried to be
An adult, responsible.'

You tried to be
But being is
Being is what you are.

'But religion is
Religion is
What is religion?

Religion is belief and group communion
Is what I had
Is what I sought.'

Taking off his toga
And revealing his gear
The prosecution says

Ah, the LCD?
Then why not mescalin?
Or the LSD?

'Not my generation,
I'm afraid,' he says.
'Not my generation.'

Chimpanzees Are Blameless Creatures

They spend most of their time eating
Or looking for food: i.e. working.

Or if they aren't messing about in trees
Or absent-mindedly

Pushing off their children
They groom each other
With great concentration
Eating the salt: i.e. loving.

They're a bit promiscuous.
They share mates comfortably
Without getting angry
And if a row breaks out
It's for no apparent reason
And suddenly ends without
Anybody being hurt.

They cuddle and touch each other a lot
And there's much
Curiosity in their sex.

Sometimes a mother will want to
Join another group:
There's a fair amount of
Shifting around.

She feels very shy about it
And the new males
Look her over
Without tension.
Then she kisses someone's hand
And someone shakes hers.
She goes round
Shaking and kissing hands
And she's part of the group.
No one makes much fuss.

Chimpanzees are blameless creatures
And it's only if they're frightened
That they'll tear your cheek off.

Billy's Book

I'm going to ask you to get up out of your seat
And say your prayers for the first time
Without thinking you know good and evil, or the difference.

I'm going to ask you to get up out of your seat
And say, after me, if God didn't exist
The Church would be necessary.

I'm going to ask you to get up out of your seat
And admit to yourself for the first time that God
Actually created and fashioned the sexual organs.

I'm going to ask you to get up out of your seat
And live entirely in the present from now on,
Renouncing both yesterday and tomorrow.

I'm going to ask you to get up out of your seat,
Walk out of this hall
And never listen to another preacher.

I'm going to ask you to get up out of your seat
And admit that God is everywhere,
Even here with Billy in Earls Court.

I'm going to ask you to get up out of your seat
And say my faith in God is such
That I renounce all idols, including my ideas about God.

I'm going to ask you to get up out of your seat,
Recognize that women are longing to give life,
And look at them in the tube train.

I'm going to ask you to get up out of your seat
And think that Billy Graham, Kosygin, Wilson, Johnson and
    De Gaulle
May well be manifestations of original sin.

I'm going to ask you to get up out of your seat
And decide whether you really want all homosexuals,
Jews, communists, Germans and suchlike to go to Hell.

I'm going to ask you to get up out of your seat,
Stay out of your seat, and try to manage without a seat
For the rest of eternity.

I'm going to ask you to get up out of your seat.

The Underground Revolution

Beer bottles are getting broken
In Holborn and Camden Town.
At this moment
In King's Road and Covent Garden
Thousands of Indian shamen
Are breaking beer bottles.

At this moment
Just off Sloane Square
The squaws are on the warpath
And thousands of Indian shamen
Are breaking beer bottles
In Notting Hill Gate.

This revolution in consciousness
Happened on the fourth dimension
When thousands of Indian shamen
Murdered in America
Walked into Blake's London
And started living in the houses.

With their superior agelessness
All those Red Indian guides
Who appeared so inexplicably
In the Spiritualist Movement
Are breaking beer bottles
Near Charing Cross Road.

Englishmen, disguised as Americans,
Wiped out the wigwam,
And now the Red Men, disguised as Englishmen,
Are coming down to Holborn,
Breaking beer bottles
And smoking pot.

You can't put new pot into old bottles,
But the tribes are coming back,
Educating the white man,
Breaking his beer bottles,
And thousands of Indian shamen
Are creating an empire, gently.

Gently they are coming down
As the so-called young,
As the sons of Albion
And the daughters of Beulah,
In clouds of weird smoke
They are breaking the beer bottles.

The News

Two men were shot in Sloane Square
This morning
When a masked queer
Invaded a bank.
One died, the newsmen think.

Miss Jayne Mansfield, the star,
Died today
When her car
Collided with the beyond.
Miss Mansfield was a blonde.

And Primo Carnera also died
This morning,
It has been verified.
He was said to be
The biggest prizefighter in history.

The Rolling Stones denied
This morning
That they had lied
About the burning incense.
It wasn't to make the hemp-smell less intense.

The Rolling Stones also avowed
This morning
That the girl hadn't allowed
The rug to slip purposely.
She had just had a bath and was waiting to dry.

And the first British Reinforcements
This morning
Arrived at encampments
In Aden by jet.
None of them are dead yet.

He Couldn't Understand Why They Locked Him Up

What he was after was the childish imaginative clarity
The schizophrenic vision
Of cool flowers lifting petals like ears
To listen to the sun, or blind eyelids
To be stroked by sunlight,
Fingers of sun
On blind eyelids, petals, lips, leaves.

But this was eccentric, and he was taught
The clarity that others sought.
And as imagination grew more powerful
The abstract fantastical
Metal and skyscraper contraption
Of petrol, steam and gears
Became the real, and only the flowers
Seemed fantastical, only the dream
Worth creating an asylum for.

All illusion: the flowers stopped listening
Because too few were imagining,
And the computers walked in
Wearing surgical aprons and sharp faces,
And people's noses grew fingers like clocks,
And once, with plugs on his head
And wired to the wall,
He coiled like a spring,
And, in a special bed,
An electric nurse struck his head with rocks.

Anna Lovell

Blues To Be There

What when the sun flies across the sallow land
When the chill sound of death approaches

When the light withdraws to warm other fingers
And shrivelled eyes turn slowly to explore

The vacillating continents that dance for hands
Beating rhythms false as decaying flesh

The sad mist curls insidiously round
And carries me away into a phantom winter

For all this year we have waited for the summer
The long brazen orgy of sun and sated smiles

But too long – there will never be another
A limbo land indeterminate and melancholy

The yellowing eyes roll back beyond the fickle sand
The soft barred edges of a nothingness

And when the chill wind blows,
What then my love?

– I will chip like a tea bell
Every silence I make

And when the sea no longer flows
My love?

– I will build a tower to reach the sky
And in it place many things
On which to grow my thoughts

And when the music is no more?

– I will shape a silence spherical and golden
From each chip until
All is perfect

And when the world sings?

– I will die.

Hydra Night Song

Throbbing electric wires
The candle spits
A spider creaks in the rush matting
Cicadas turn over in their sleep
The wind under the door
A donkey brays
The mountains echo
A mule shuffling up the road
An old woman wheezing like a tired ghost
A cat skittering from the rubbish
My heart beats
The paraffin glass contracts
Water boils on the fire
Radio static
Pen patterns
My finger through my hair

A cough
A little plaster falls in the room above
Some furniture settling
A falling star where it meets the sea.

Loneliness

No breeze touches skin
no sea waves tease feet
no fishes catch the eye
no birds in the hair
no sun heats the blood
no silk smooths limbs
no sweet words stroke the ear
no love within the heart
no smile at the corners of the mouth
no meat within the belly
no hashish in the pipe
no stars in the sky
no secret in the mind
no night in the dark
no day in the light
no season between ice and fire
no moment in time
no arrival in any place
no magic in meeting
no seeing in looking
no hearing in listening
no feeling in touching
no knowing in understanding
there are further continents

There is a place for wisdom yet.

Paul Matthews

'I touch you in secret ways'

The lightbulb sings, vibrating
at a speed that is God to me.
The fly knows it, dying there
in electric rage. I am naked.
I transmit love across continents
to my Spanish lady.
                          She writes –
'I danced in the village square. My blood
does not flow with the music,
though last year it was everything.'

My love, I teach you
to dance the NOW, the electric body. First
you must touch me.

She writes of a storm – '3 hours
of rose coloured flashes. We hid
in the furthest room.'

I too know the lightning. In its shapes
I recognize Gods fucking.
Run to it girl, undress, touch
me – you must die for love.

Michael McCafferty

City Poem

(this poem is for those who know the proper time and the proper dress
   for the place to be
And knowing this devote their steps to the city's dance.)

This here now city
thirty two hands
fingers casually trace the borders
lines the resting places of these families
where the robber baron pinned to his chest
six hundred years ago this strip of pavement
now that I walk.
Perspectives are Zoom lens the mind uses
to this city inside
where the banks are

          Slow time
          the eyes movement
          then follows
          the umbrella
          the bulging briefcase
          the face above the old school tie
It hasn't changed much these last ten years
a Yardley fragrance perhaps replaces the smell of thyme

From an upstairs window in St Johns Wood
or the top of the Millbank tower with narrowed eyes
the city world like Kew gardens
is flat, ordered, labelled,
the direction of growth observed,
and cultured on the best of all possible soils.

But from here
this point on the street
in the night
these skies are blue
in the stillness
these trees are shaped
my footsteps now at this hour
make small indentations on the concrete
a quickness moves in the centre of my body
as my slow time on the streets reveals another world
a world of people who say
it's getting a bit cold
when they mean
close the fucking door
and everyone has two spoons of sugar in their tea
They feed the birds/would never
dream of suggesting a jukebox in the Vatican
or laying out plastic skeletons
for the destruction or amusement of vultures
but will if asked politely
explore a deserted house in Acklam road
                    or any other road
                Languidly dwelling on the metaphysics of
                                        [dwellings
A man who has worked all his life for a £1000 pound in the
                            bank and a house to die in
Must to all seen understood read
and I who may think his bottle a bit damp
still have to contend with his sociological attitudes.
While these people slur their tracks across the pavement
the tame eagle sits and waits
the city waits eternally
all dreams of conquest
find dust strained through muslin

washed by the rain
drained to the sea
the ever devoured
eternally renewed city
on the seas finger
metalless in a kind light
a virgin awaits awakening by its destroyer.

John McGrath

Prologue to 'Why the Chicken?'

(To be spoken by a crusty old park keeper who wanders into a broken-down farmhouse. In the background gleam the sky scrapers and regular rows of houses of a brand new 'new town'.)

Yobble de hoo. Dare we mar again. What an iffley slape. An all dese young leople hopping all over de flower-debs. Ug. I spedise young leople. Infinitely I obnegate um. Gad! Im dey tum, whisk over de tunkry side, lobble awong, shtur it up, no end they do, op, op! fie on dem! Oh oh oh fie on dem again! De unterpinitrability of dese ungsters is invincible, ich can only itch and wonder dey gon't die of ut. Loaf means onthing oo tem. Why? Agos loaf is a spleny-wendored wing oo oo, yes, an dey no onting off it. Piserable ungsters, danksters dey are, no loaf, no liff, lony bahbah, und ping ping und tse-tse, und ta und ta und ta, no ta. Ug. Fie on dem. Un doose flot is it? Dem's not we's. Dem make murk along. Dem catchastrongers, flooming tikiotic, brawnding, roaring, broom broom broom broom, ikey-botors, broom broom unt SMASH or SQUASH dall ay. Oo oo. Fie on dem. Not us. We'm de buzzy biddies, flugling adown all day, edifying monstructions, oobling mouses, poo tlive in, ook, ook, nike leople, ook at de mouses we oobled por dem. Und loaf we have por dem, oops und oops of loaf por dem, toe much loaf perpraps, tub loaf inweed we have, fennything, menny-thing, rennything, dey grab we got we give. Oops of loaf. Dem esposed dig us like – a crazy. Do dey?

Do dey duck egg your margin, imsis, egg your margin,
urse, ich get otched off away, noo noo.

Plojamies. Ping.
Plowmen. Drover my boulder goes one share;
vair vair ve? Ich vas vambling no und no und no
waboo dey unksters. Ug. Foo! Fie on dem.

Ich gonna tellya tale. Oh pot a wail! Lormost a sad
assa long strong dear trop umptling inna bowla soop.
Oh oo oh. Vot a sty was vair. Ve'm de kiddies
vot oobled veryting.

Ta debing vit: we'm da kiddies vot blooed it all
uuup! All dat russhib. Blooed it all pie-sigh.
Agos twas robble. Horroble. Oo many twouses,
oo many eeple, nog enug grass, nog enug spatse,
nog enug land oo tlive on. Tub *ve* dign't leebensroom
shout! Oh doe oh doe ear me doe doedoe. Agos
Tiggler shotted dat, und boom boom tvas drabstruction.
Ve'm da kiddies vot bilt up da vunderbar noo tizzies,
nowts, tummunities. Vot ya tink abou da, eh?
A ndwen ve blit a noo nowts und tizzies und tummunities,
ook, dere dey yare! (*points to set*) den auf auf auf o
dem ole louses, de nowts, inta da noo wins, i' vos a
try-umph. Uvly uvly: da ole wans vos robble, horroble,
now dey rubble, hurruble, like dis ear, ug, iffley slape.
Ve all got um oo voms, snise. Tub vot da bruttle is
is dis Da unksters. Dey treble bruttle. Da unksters
dey'm danksters, dey'm dinjusted mitta noo vons, dey
wun marred. Ich bin bruttly mangry mittum. Ve'm
all be bruttly mangry agos dey doan per-reeseate i' a–
tall. Dey'm ignrateful. Ug. Bruttle. Tebruttle.
Ich bin trebly mangry, an dey hop all over da flower-
debs. Oo oo oo. Ich doan diggum, no' a' or: ich undiggum.

Song

And when our streets are green again
When metalled roads are green
And girls walk barefoot through the weeds
Of Regent Street, Saint Martin's Lane

And children hide in factories
Where burdock blooms and vetch and rust,
And elms and oaks and chestnut trees
Are tall again, and hope is lost

When up the Strand the foxes glide
And hedgehogs sniff and wildcats yell
And golden orioles come back
To flash through Barnes and Clerkenwell

When governments and industries
Lie choked by weeds in fertile rain
For sure the few who stay alive
Will laugh and grow to love again

Tom McGrath

Benzedrine

So uneasy   about going to sleep,
you would think my skull
would welcome a pillow
and some easing of its vigilance
      at least
but no it stays up
rigid and watching
and if it droops for a moment
it jerks straight back
anxious to prove its not a flower
      maybe
and is as durable as the next skull.
What the hell is it waiting for?

Look, I tell it, the next skull is asleep
and the rest of me is anxious
to move in warm beside her on the sheets
and melt away for a few hours. Why
      the hell should you tell my big toe
it can't sleep?

Eventually the head gets flabby,
eyes hood over, deep enclose yawns
from the mouth. The skull surrenders
and the rest of me staggers
towards the bed and she
who is maybe nightmaring.

In bed at last, at last the time
to sleep, at last, at last.
She is breathing slow and deep
beside me. I move in at her body
and stay there like seaweed. At
last.

A moment. Darkness. Another moment.
Breathing. My toes start wiggling.
I have a hard-on. I am wide awake.

The Evidence

*This poem was set in motion by a strange mixture of informations: there was
the revulsion I felt at the Vietnam war scene and the admiration I felt for
Sukarno's concept of the New Emerging Forces. Mal Caldwell, a learned,
hairy Scotsman, had just returned from Indonesia. He said that there was an
air of expectancy, an idea of future, about that country, despite its faults,
which was terribly absent in England. Just at that time, though, Sukarno was
denouncing jazz and the Beatles. I didn't go for that much. Mal passed me a
learned book – 'Africa and Indonesia: the evidence of the xylophone and
other musical and cultural factors' by A. M. Jones – which set out a proof
that African culture was influenced at a very early stage by visiting Indonesians
– particularly African music. Africa to America gave jazz. Beatles picked up on
American jazz-based sounds to make their pop music blues. The Beatles
sound goes to Indonesia and Sukarno says no. Wow! I wanted to tell him
something that his politics had made him miss. Eric Dolphy, the sax player,
was dead when this poem was written. I had just heard the news and was
upset by it. He is an appropriate musician to quote at Sukarno because of the
Afro-Asian sounds that he often employed, so naturally, in his music. I don't
suppose I need to explain who Bird Parker was, so that's the references
covered. My personal life also gets involved in this poem: I have great difficulty
in relating what happens to me with what is happening to some unfortunate in
Vietnam. Yet I am sure there is a definite connexion.*
This poem was first read at the Albert Hall reading, June 1965.
At this point you begin to listen :

the climate is changing, the wind etc
sweeps a continent, revolutions
in the undergrowth, Indonesia
she loves the soft paper touch of survival:
I am crazy for the feel of her wombanity,
but there is no money in my pocket
and anyway I have a wife on my arm.
a woman to love, if not exclusively,
at least with some claims to continuity,
      a love, a life –
      time is not enough
      to love as the human should
      to keep the peace in
      the Vietnams out, the world
      and the xylophone

              maybe if Johnson had Sukarno's
                women . . . maybe that is
              the Asian threat . . . the South
              all over again . . . the Indonesian
              will take our women . . . the evidence
              the evidence,
              hear it out there,
              the African birds are squawking,
              climate changing, the wind etc.

              Sukarno, Sukarno, you had no right
              to say no to Dolphy.
              He played the sounds of your old
                            new world.

My personal realities
against your politicalities,
cocks against the bomb. Life is good,
life is good, when will I listen to my own prayers?

Atrocity pictures, meester? You want
cunt with your curry?

            Vietnam, Vietnam. Life and a man.
            You said it: a nightmare.

Just then Mal came in
drunk and learned. Go away, Mal,
and let me sleep. No xylophones
here.

            'The Vietnamese women are . . .'
            He raised his arm
            in phallic appreciation.
            'The Vietnamese women are . . .'
            In his randy face
            a vision
            of peace
            that's a new tune they're playing tonight,
            are you afraid of that music? Hey,
            Sukarno, listen – the evidence
            of the xylophone.

You said it: only a dream.
Tumble off the bed, bellyfull of curry,
tongue dry, arse heavy, thoughts heavy
with thoughts
of war –

Someone somewhere wants a bombing from you.
Atrocity pictures, meester?

At this point no defining
what the war is
unless you are the son
who sees his father blown up
for the sake of a bar of American chocolate,

then there's knowledge of sorts
but no saying of it.

                Vietnam, Vietnam, Vietnam.

God that curry was hot.
An hour ago the intensity of hunger
ripped my stomach, too many cigarettes,
a headache but a reality at least;
now it's move over, shut up
and let me sleep.
                Vietnam. Viet-nam. Vie et man.
                Life and a rose and a thorn,
                the Sacred Heart symbols
                bleed out too easy. Hey,
                Sukarno, why don't you
                blow the fuck out of Johnson?
                The evidence of the xylophone,
                Sukarno. You can't put a ban
                on Bird Parker.

The whore I met in Soho,
sitting on top of a dustbin of all things,
smiling and calling to the men going past,

endearingly, but not endearing enough
supposedly – the men are embarrassed,
for God's sake,
                  embraced maybe, yes,
she transmits visions of cock,
dark rooms, trousers crumpled on the floor,
myself beside her, tickling the tips of her breasts
                  with fivers

Before You Sleep
(*written after Albert Hall poetry reading, June 1965*)

move over and I'll tell you why
the poets wont bring revolutions
of love and flowers and poetry:

its because most poets are egotists,
gross egotists, who are really a bit sad
that other poets exist

but are glad so many flowers exist
to pour out sutras and elegies over
and prove this poet's so good
he can even match the beauty of a flower

and glad of course that poetry was around
when they discovered that after all
they would not make it as a philosopher
or a holyman or a jazz musician or a painter
or the mightiest lover or the politician

poetry was around to sustain them
with the power dreams proffered
by the word

Move closer and I'll tell you about the poet
who was always writing love poems about his marvels
with his angel woman in bed:

you know, all the time he was writing
she was making it with a store detective.

Stuart Mills

Sending Out A Prophet

I have bought you a white suit
to match your eyes,
and a white hat to shade them from the sun.

You must drive fast along wide roads
and stop only at the towns
I have indicated on the map.

Here is money for your expenses.

In the Low Countries

They are building a ship
in a field;
bigger than I should have thought
sensible.
When it is finished
there will never be enough of them
to carry it to the sea.
And already
it's turning rusty.

Ted Milton

Coleman's 'Tomorrow is the Question'

Rubber notes
through an apricot dawn,
Look below!
A suspension bridge
of the bass's diving music;
how they play
like airborne dolphins,
at the same time aware
of a drum's authority.
Be alert!
Their genius
may catch you
tapping your feet
at an obsolete tempo!

Waiting in The Tate
(*The Nation's most costly waiting room.*)

Standing before a pale copy of my own head & shoulders
        which has for its background
        a restless throng
        in search of one
        which'll really hold them
        this time for good,

Watching a doomed girl shuffling slowly across
        till she's finally consumed
        in wood & wall,

Tense anticipating trouble from the uniform
>   who's being paid
>   specifically to wait
>   to move in on the attack
>   on behalf of the Masters,

Hearing small comments all around falling & floating,

Angry with the Board of Governors for overheating this place,

Angry with myself for having on too many clothes
>   before a J. M. W. Turner

In the long wait for his sun to melt the glass
>   burn all backdrops
>   dissolve all sitters
>   set for good.

Siesta

A mosquito
motors in the room,

a taxi
in the ghost town.

Somewhere
saloon doors
creak in the wind.

Poem of a Would-Be Flyer

You untouchables barely discernible in the back seats of taxis
        borne gently along by the worn & musty leather –

Your thoughts remain behind dark glass as you're ferried to
        the skyscraper/where a scarlet doorman waits to rush
        forward to adjust your furs/ & 'Monsieur Madame'
        you across the whispering foyer/to the humming
        lift.

On the hundredth floor
        the cage doors slide quietly open onto the plush decor
        & a statuesque waiter relieves you of your coats.

As the orchestra serenades
        you cross to the window with a sigh of relief
        at last able to breathe fresh air
        & savour a drink.

Cool breezes caressing your foreheads
        you're as elevated as a cruising jet
        high above this city
        winking beneath.

You take a glance out
        & see a silent galaxy.

The Dependable Salmon

It is the Dependable Salmon
who is on guard.

Chippendale heirlooms
clutter the room.

With a massive salute
 & newly polished presented arms
he is maintaining the blockade
without any foreign aid.

Sharp windows
sever the air.

But the regal Clan of Cow
will come home soon,
 & play musical chairs.

Trusty old Salmon
hasn't a care.

I Want None of Miss Joan Hunter Dunne, Because

I long for the Little Miss Smith
though I know she has the mind of a sieve

but it is made of pure silver

where all day she is sifting her dream
of a new life on the carpeted cliff.

Truly it would be bliss
to live with you Miss –

I would even buy you a solid mahogany kitchen counter
I would even buy you an authenticated Japanese ivory sink.

'The Creature stood there'

The creature stood there
With his hands on the bear –
Where is your lever? he cried –
If you reach down inside
You never know what you may find –
It may even have hairs.

O the silvery pines
Stood together that night,
Not to say that they were untied –
No, but they were, deep down inside.

Adrian Mitchell

Veteran With A Head Wound

Nothing to show for it at first
But dreams and shivering, a few mistakes.
Shapes lounged around his mind chatting of murder,
Telling interminable jokes,
Watching like tourists for Vesuvius to burst.

He started listening. Too engrossed to think,
He let his body move in jerks,
Talked just to prove himself alive, grew thin,
Lost five jobs in eleven weeks,
Then started drinking, blamed it on the drink.

He'd seen a woman, belly tattered, run
Her last yards. He had seen a fat
Friend roll in flames, as if his blood were paraffin,
And herded enemies, waiting to be shot,
Stand looking straight into the sun.

They couldn't let him rot in the heat
In the corner of England like a garden chair.
A handy-man will take a weathered chair,
Smooth it, lay on a glowing layer
Of paint and tie a cushion to the seat.

They did all anyone could do –
Tried to grate off the colour of his trouble,
Brighten him up a bit. His rare
Visitors found him still uncomfortable.
The old crimson paint showed through.

Each night he heard from the back of his head,
As he was learning to sleep again,
Funny or terrible voices tell
Or ask him how their deaths began.
These are the broadcasts of the dead.

One voice became a plaintive bore.
It could only remember the grain and shine
Of a wooden floor, the forest smell
Of its fine surface. The voice rasped on
For hours about that pretty floor.

'If I could make that floor again,'
The voice insisted, over and over,
'The floor on which I died,' it said,
'Then I could stand on it for ever
Letting the scent of polish lap my brain.'

He became Boswell to the dead.
In cruel script their deaths are written.
Generously they are fed
In that compound for the forgotten,
His crowded, welcoming head.

The doctors had seen grimmer cases.
They found his eyes were one-way mirrors,
So they could easily look in
While he could only see his terrors,
Reflections of those shuttered faces.

Stepping as far back as I dare,
(For the man may stagger and be broken
Like a bombed factory or hospital).
I see his uniform is woven
Of blood, bone, flesh and hair.

Populated by the simple dead,
This soldier, in his happy dreams,
Is killed before he kills at all.
Bad tenant that he is, I give him room;
He is the weeper in my head.

Since London's next bomb will tear
Her body in its final rape,
New York and Moscow's ashes look the same
And Europe go down like a battleship,
Why should one soldier make me care?

Ignore him or grant him a moment's sadness.
He walks the burning tarmac road
To the asylum built with bricks of flame.
Abandon him and you must make your own
House of incinerating madness.

The horizon is only paces away.
We walk an alley through a dark,
Criminal city. None can pass.
We would have to make love, fight or speak
If we met someone travelling the other way.

A tree finds its proportions without aid.
Dogs are not tutored to be fond.
Penny-size frogs traverse the grass
To the civilization of a pond.
Grass withers yearly, is re-made.

Trees become crosses because man is born.
Dogs may be taught to shrink from any hand.
Dead frogs instruct the scientist,
Spread clouds of poison in the pond –
You kill their floating globes of spawn.

In London, where the trees are lean,
The banners of the grass are raised.
Grass feeds the butcher and the beast,
But we could conjure down a blaze
Would scour the world of the colour green.

For look, though the human soul is tough,
Our state scratches itself in bed
And a thousand are pierced by its fingernails.
It combs its hair, a thousand good and bad
Fall away like discs of dandruff.

For a moment it closes its careful fist
And, keening for the world of streets,
More sons of God whisper in jails
Where the unloved the unloved meet.
The days close round them like a dirty mist.

When death covers England with a sheet
Of red and silver fire, who'll mourn the state,
Though some will live; and some bear children
And some of the children born in hate
May be both lovely and complete?

Try to distract this soldier's mind
From his distraction. Under the powdered buildings
He lies alive, still shouting,
With his brothers and sisters and perhaps his children,
While we bury all the dead people we can find.

Nostalgia – Now Threepence Off

Where are they now, the heroes of furry-paged books and
comics brighter than life which packed my ink-lined desk in
days when BOP meant Boys' Own Paper, where are they any-
way?

Where is Percy F. Westerman? Where are H. L. Gee and
Arthur Mee? Where is Edgar Rice (The Warlord of Mars)
Burroughs, the Bumper Fun Book and the Wag's Handbook?
Where is the Wonder Book of Reptiles? Where the hell is
The Boy's Book of Bacteriological Warfare?

Where are the Beacon Readers? Did Ro-ver, that tireless
hound, devour his mon-o-syll-ab-ic-all-y correct family? Did
Little Black Sambo and Epaminondas shout for 'Black Power'?

Did Peter Rabbit get his when myxomatosis came round the
second time, did the Flopsy Bunnies stiffen to a standstill, grow
bug-eyed, fly-covered and then disintegrate?

Where is G. A. Henty and his historical lads – Wolfgang the
Hittite, Armpit the Young Viking, Cyril who lived in Sodom?
Where are their uncorrupted bodies and Empire-building
brains, England needs them, the Sunday Times says so.

There is news from the Strewelpeter mob. Johnny-Head-In-
Air spends his days reporting flying saucers, the telephone
receiver never cools from the heat of his hand. Little Harriet,
who played with matches, still burns, but not with fire. The
Scissorman is everywhere.

Babar the Elephant turned the jungle into a garden city.
But things went wrong. John and Susan, Titty and Roger,
became unaccountably afraid of water, sold their dinghies, all
married each other, live in a bombed-out cinema on surgical
spirits and weeds of all kinds.

Snow White was in the News of the World – Virgin Lived
With Seven Midgets, Court Told. And in the psychiatric ward

an old woman dribbles as she mumbles about a family of human bears, they ate porridge, yes Miss Goldilocks of course they did.

Hans Brinker vainly whirled his silver skates round his head as the jackboots of Emil and the Detectives invaded his Resistance cellar.

Some failed. Desperate Dan and Meddlesome Matty and Strang the Terrible and Korky the Cat killed themselves with free gifts in a back room at the Peter Pan Club because they were impotent, like us. Their audience, the senile chums of Red Circle School, still wearing for reasons of loyalty and lust the tatters of their uniforms, voted that exhibition a super wheeze.

Some succeeded. Tom Sawyer's heart has cooled, his ingenuity flowers at Cape Kennedy.

But they are all trodden on, the old familiar faces, so at the rising of the sun and the going down of the ditto I remember I remember the house where I was taught to play up play up and play the game though nobody told me what the game was, but we know now, don't we, we know what the game is, for lives of great men all remind us we can make our lives sublime and departing leave behind us arseprints on the sands of time, but the tide's come up, the castles are washed down, where are they now, where are they, where are the deep shelters? There are no deep shelters. Biggles may drop it, Worrals of the Wraf may press the button. So, Billy and Bessie Bunter prepare for the last and cosmic Yarooh and throw away the Man-Tan. The sky will soon be full of suns.

Hear the Voice of the Critic

There are too many colours.
The Union Jack's all right, selective,
Two basic colours and one negative,
Reasonable, avoids confusion.
    (Of course I respect the red, white and blue)

But there are too many colours.
The rainbow, well it's gaudy, but I am
Bound to admit, a useful diagram
When treated as an optical illusion.
    (Now I'm not saying anything against rainbows)

But there are too many colours.
Take the sea. Unclassifiable.
The sky – the worst offender of all,
Tasteless as Shakespeare, especially at sunset.
    (I wish my body were all one colour).

There are too many colours.
I collect flat white plates.
You ought to see my flat white plates.
In my flat white flat I have a perfect set,
    (It takes up seven rooms).

There are too many colours.

Briefing

He may be fanatical, he may have a madness.
Either way, move carefully.
He must be surrounded, but he's contagious.

One of you will befriend his family.
One male and one female will love the subject
Until he loves you back. Gradually

Our team will abstract and collect
His mail, nail-clippings, garbage, friends, words, schemes,
Graphs of his fears, scars, sex and intellect.

Steam open his heart. Tap his dreams.
Learn him inside and inside out.
When he laughs, laugh. Scream when he screams.

He will scream. 'Innocent!' He'll shout
Until his mouth is broken with stones.
We use stones. We take him out

To a valley full of stones.
He stands against a shed. He stands on stones
Naked. The initial stones

Shower the iron shed. Those stones
Outline the subject. When he cries for stones
The clanging ceases. Then we give him stones,

Filling his universe with stones.
Stones – his atoms turn to stones
And he becomes a stone buried in stones.

A final tip. Then you may go.
Note the half-hearted stoners and watch how
Your own arm throws. And watch how I throw.

Stunted Sonnet

Love is like a cigarette –
The bigger the drag, the more you get.

Lullaby for William Blake

Blakehead, babyhead,
Your head is full of light.
You sucked the sun like a gobstopper.
Blakehead, babyhead,
High as a satellite on sunflower seeds,
First man-powered man to fly the Atlantic,
Inventor of the poem which kills itself,
The poem which gives birth to itself,
The human form, jazz, Jerusalem
And other luminous, luminous galaxies.
You out-spat your enemies.
You irradiated your friends.
Always naked, you shaven, shaking tyger-lamb,
Moon-man, moon-clown, moon-singer, moon-drinker,
You never killed anyone.
Blakehead, babyhead,
Accept this mug of crude red wine –
I love you.

You Get Used To It

*'Am I in Alabama or am I in hell?' A minister, Montgomery, Alabama,
March 1965*

Begging-bowl eyes, begging-bowl eyes,
skin round hoops of wire.
They do not eat, they are being eaten,
saw them in the papers.

But it's only bad if you know it's bad,
fish don't want the sky.
If you've spent all your life in hell or Alabama
you get used to it.

Ignorant husband, ignorant wife,
each afraid of the other one's bomb.
He spends all he has in the Gentlemen's
on a half-crown book of nudes.

But it's only bad if you know it's bad,
fish don't want the sky.
If you've spent all your life in hell or Alabama
you get used to it.

Beautiful blossom of napalm
sprouting from the jungle,
bloom full of shrivelling things,
might be mosquitoes, might be men.

But it's only bad if you know it's bad,
fish don't want the sky.
If you've spent all your life in hell or Alabama
you get used to it.

I hurt, you hurt, he hurts, she hurts,
we hurt, you hurt, they hurt.
What can't be cured must go to jail,
what can't be jailed must die.

But it's only bad if you know it's bad,
fish don't want the sky.
If you've spent all your life in hell or Alabama
you get used to it.

To Whom It May Concern

I was run over by the truth one day.
Ever since the accident I've walked this way
  So stick my legs in plaster
  Tell me lies about Vietnam.

Heard the alarm clock screaming with pain,
Couldn't find myself so I went back to sleep again
  So fill my ears with silver
  Stick my legs in plaster
  Tell me lies about Vietnam.

Every time I shut my eyes all I see is flames.
Made a marble phone book, carved all the names
  So coat my eyes with butter
  Fill my ears with silver
  Stick my legs in plaster
  Tell me lies about Vietnam.

I smell something burning, hope it's just my brains.
They're only dropping peppermints and daisy-chains
  So stuff my nose with garlic
  Coat my eyes with butter
  Fill my ears with silver
  Stick my legs in plaster
  Tell me lies about Vietnam.

Where were you at the time of the crime?
Down by the Cenotaph drinking slime
  So chain my tongue with whisky
  Stuff my nose with garlic

Coat my eyes with butter
Fill my ears with silver
Stick my legs in plaster
Tell me lies about Vietnam.

You put your bombers in, you put your conscience out,
You take the human being and you twist it all about
So scrub my skin with women
Chain my tongue with whisky
Stuff my nose with garlic
Coat my eyes with butter
Fill my ears with silver
Stick my legs in plaster
Tell me lies about Vietnam.

Norman Morrison

On November 2nd 1965
in the multi-coloured multi-minded
United beautiful States of terrible America
Norman Morrison set himself on fire
outside the Pentagon.
He was thirty-one, he was a Quaker,
and his wife (seen weeping in the newsreels)
and his three children
survive him as best they can.
He did it in Washington where everyone could see
because
people were being set on fire
in the dark corners of Vietnam where nobody could see.
Their names, ages, beliefs and loves
are not recorded.
This is what Norman Morrison did.

He poured petrol over himself.
He burned. He suffered.
He died.
That is what he did
in the white heart of Washington
where everyone could see.
He simply burned away his clothes,
his passport, his pink-tinted skin,
put on a new skin of flame
and became
Vietnamese.

To You

One: we were swaddled, ugly-beautiful and drunk on milk.
Two: cuddled in arms always covered by laundered sleeves.
Three: we got sand and water to exercise our imaginative
    faculties.
Four: we were hit. Suddenly hit.

Five: we were fed to the educational system limited.
Six: worried by the strange creatures in our heads, we strangled
    some of them.
Seven: we graduated in shame.
Eight: World War Two, and we hated the Germans as much
    as our secret bodies, loved the Americans as much as the
    Russians, hated killing, loved killing, depending on the
    language in the Bible in the breast pocket of the dead
    soldier, we were crazy-thirsty for Winston Superman, for
    Jesus with his infinite tommy-gun and the holy Spitfires,
    while the Jap dwarfs hacked through the undergrowth
    of our nightmares – there were pits full of people-meat –

and the real bombs came, but they didn't hit us, my love,
   they didn't hit us exactly.
My love, they are trying to drive us mad.

So we got to numbers eight, nine, ten, eleven,
Growing scales over every part of our bodies,
Especially our eyes,
Because scales were being worn, because scales were armour.
And now we stand, past thirty, together, madder than ever.
We make a few diamonds and lose them.
We sell our crap by the ton.
My love, they are trying to drive us mad.

Make love. We must make love
Instead of making money.
You know about rejection? Hit. Suddenly hit.
Want to spend my life building poems in which untamed
People and animals walk around freely, lie down freely,
Make love freely
In the deep loving carpets, stars circulating in the ceiling,
Poems like honeymoon planetariums.
But our time is burning.
My love, they are trying to drive us mad.

Peace was all I ever wanted.
It was too expensive.
My love, they are trying to drive us mad.

Half the people I love are shrinking.
My love, they are trying to drive us mad.

Half the people I love are exploding.
My love, they are trying to drive us mad.

I am afraid of going mad.

To The Statues in Poets' Corner,
Westminster Abbey

You stony bunch of pockskinned whiteys,
Why kip in here? Who sentenced you?
They are buying postcards of you,
The girls in safety knickers.
Tombfaces, glumbums,
Wine should be jumping out of all your holes,
You should have eyes that roll, arms that knock things over,
Legs that falter and working cocks.
Listen.
On William Blake's birthday we're going to free you,
Blast you off your platforms with a blowtorch full of brandy
And then we'll all stomp over to the Houses of Parliament
And drive them into the Thames with our bananas.

To a Russian soldier in Prague

You are going to be hated by the people.

They will hate you over their freakish breakfast of tripe soup
  and pastries.
They will squint hatred at you on their way to pretend to work.
By the light of yellow beer they will hate you with jokes you'll
  never hear.

You are beginning to feel
Like a landlord in a slum.
Like a white man in Harlem.
Like a US Marine in Saigon.

T—CA—H

Socialists are hated
By all who kill for profit and power.
But you are going to be hated by
The people – who are all different.
The people – who are all extraordinary.
The people – who are all of equal value.
Socialism is theirs, it was invented for them.
Socialism is theirs, it can only be made by them.

Africa, Asia, and Latin America are screaming:
STARVATION. POVERTY. OPPRESSION.
When they turn to America
They see only flames and children in the flames
When they turn to England
They see an old lady in a golden wheelchair,
Share certificates in one hand, a pistol in the other.
When they turn to Russia
They see – you.

You are going to be hated
As the English have usually been hated.
The starving, the poor, and the oppressed
Are turning, turning away.
While you nervously guard a heap of documents,
They stagger away through the global crossfire
Towards revolution, towards socialism.

Leaflets
(For Brian Patten and my twelve students at Bradford College of Art)

Outside the plasma supermarket
I stretch out my arm to the shoppers and say:
'Can I give you one of these?'

I give each of them a leaf from a tree.

The first shopper thanks me.
The second puts the leaf in his mack pocket where his wife
    won't see.
The third says she is not interested in leaves. She looks like a
    mutilated willow.
The fourth says: 'Is it art?' I say that it is a leaf.
The fifth looks through his leaf and smiles at the light beyond.
The sixth hurls down his leaf and stamps it till dark purple mud
    oozes through.
The seventh says she will press it in her album.
The eighth complains that it is an oak leaf and says he would be
    on my side if I were also handing out birch leaves,
    apple leaves, privet leaves and larch leaves. I say that
    it is a leaf.
The ninth takes the leaf carefully and then, with a backhand
    fling, gives it its freedom.
It glides, following surprise curving alleys through the air.
It lands. I pick it up.
The tenth reads both sides of the leaf twice and then says: 'Yes,
    but it doesn't say who we should kill.'

But you took your leaf like a kiss.

They tell me that, on Saturdays,
You can be seen in your own city centre
Giving away forests, orchards, jungles.

Edwin Morgan

The Death of Marilyn Monroe

What innocence? Whose guilt? What eyes? Whose breast?
Crumpled orphan, nembutal bed,
white hearse, Los Angeles,
DiMaggio! Los Angeles! Miller! Los Angeles! America!
That Death should seem the only protector –
That all arms should have faded, and the great cameras and
      lights become an inquisition and a torment –
That the many acquaintances, the autograph-hunters, the in-
      flexible directors, the drive-in admirers should become a
      blur of incomprehension and pain –
That lonely Uncertainty should limp up, grinning, with be-
      wildering barbiturates, and watch her undress and lie
      down and in her anguish
call for him! call for him to strengthen her with what could
      only dissolve her! A method
of dying, we are shaken, we see it. Strasberg!
Los Angeles! Olivier! Los Angeles! Others die
and yet by this death we are a little shaken, we feel it,
America.
Let no one say communication is a cantword.
They had to lift her hand from the bedside telephone.
But what she had not been able to say
perhaps she had said. 'All I had was my life.
I have no regrets, because if I made
any mistakes, I was responsible.
There is now – and there is the future.
What has happened is behind. So
it follows you around? So what?' – This

to a friend, ten days before.
And so she was responsible.
And if she was not responsible, not wholly responsible, Los
    Angeles? Los Angeles? Will it follow you around? Will
    the slow white hearse of the child of America follow you
    around?

For the International Poetry Incarnation
Royal Albert Hall, 11 June 1965

Worldscene! Worldtime! Spacebreaker! Wildship! Starman!
Gemini man dangles white and golden – the world floats
on a gold cord and curves blue white beautiful below him –
Vostok shrieks and prophesies, Mariner's prongs flash –
to the wailing of Voskhod Earth sighs, she shakes men loose at
    last –
out, in our time, to be living seeds sent far beyond
even imagination, though imagination is awake – take
poets on your voyages! Prometheus
embraces Icarus and in a gold shell with wings
he launches him up through the ghostly detritus
of gods and dirty empires and dying laws,
he mounts, he cries, he shouts, he shines, he streams
like light new done, his home is in a sun
and he shall be the burning unburned one.
In darkness, Daedalus
embraces Orpheus, the dark lips caked with earth and roots
he kisses open, the cold body he rubs
to a new life – the dream
flutters in a cage of crumbling bars, reviving

and then beginning slowly singing of the stars.

Beginning singing, born to go.
To cut the cord of gold. To get
the man new born to go.

Without It

Without it
there is nothing, an emptiness that's broken
by a nail scraping a drum, you cower in the hole of the drum
    screaming, no one hears you, sees you,
the space is empty to the eaves, the eaves to the stars,
an electronic yelling from Andromeda
hits the dish, how you subsist, the waves hideous to your hunger
    bang you flat to the hard black drum wall
standing, standing screaming, spreadeagled, revolving
with no hand in yours on either side of the slipping wall
and falling, never fallen, you subsist
cast out, cast into your cast iron maiden
who cannot kill, you subsist on the spikes
of anti-matter till you're cast in cries,
and no one hears, or sees, and the star
sends, and sends, and sends
unsteady, monstrous, waning
vacant until it dies, you'd give a world
for a stream of human lies,
because they could be lies.

(And you remember
diving in the pool together, flashing through the dapple
with the leaves trailing, never dreamed
there could be such pleasure, while the great wheel
bent its business to break you,
a thunderstorm scattered the flying heels

and trains and letters and bad faith and time
corrupted the heart, and one day there was nothing
as if, like the old stories, it had never been.)

Grinding rotor! Grave of dreams! Children
play on the sands you plunge through,
a desolation without dimension.
The swallow builds in your invisible eaves,
and poppies linger blowing long,
the smell of miles of acrid iron seems far away.
But everything is in its place, the pinch of clover
from a summer field could break the heart.
Subsist in iron, and wait.

Tina Morris

'In the beginning, they selected a site'

In the beginning they selected a site
where sun & wind & rain
would not penetrate for it was to be
a beautiful garden they were making.
to please their god.
A garden with flowers which bloomed
at the touch of a switch. & trees,
not too small & not too tall,
which would not lose their leaves
in autumn. And many unusual colourful
plants. and fans to create a fresh spring breeze.

The garden was full of light
so that the beauty of the flowers would be
always visible. to their god.
& soft grass aired by underground heating
where he could recline to watch
the coloured lights in the water-fall
& listen to the music playing perpetually.
to soothe their god.
On invisible wires they hung flying creatures
of many colours. & on the grass placed stuffed deer
& on the glass lake, swans.

Then they began creating their god.

'The mad musicman'

The mad musicman
is hammering again
at the window of our world.
his eyes wild peering
thru wind/rain/frenzy
thru/into the peaceful
green of our spring.
Out there all is madness
& terror & strange beasts
lurk in shadow. & the sun
wears a hangman's noose.
& fingers are severed from all hands
& no dreams anywhere.

His thin rattling fingers
tapping with wind/hail
against glass.

we lie close/cool in day's twilight
& allow the outside world
to become but a memory
in our arms

From 'Journeys/Cages'

The ring spinning slowly round, golden/green/blue/red/
yellow, sparkling with lustre. a gigantic catherine wheel
spluttering out a million shades & hues. spinning faster &
faster, carrying him into its fervid revolutions until he was no
more than a speck of colour vibrating with the rest. round &

round & the ring expanding to embrace the outside world. the outside becoming inside. the whole spinning like a massive musical top into the colours of the sky. Throwing out specks of colour which sounded as musical notes. & forming a long ecstatic melody with the whole. His arms thrown wide & his mouth open – to embrace/swallow the sound of colours. He was a prism. a chromatic scale. spinning lightly into a con-centric fluorescent world of sound. Colours were flowing out from his body. & into his body. vibrating & pulsating into an opaque circle of Colour. colours daubed together like an untidy palette, & forming not separate spectrums but a united flush of radiance.

Music rippled thru the movement: piano trills & flickers. A rhythm of breathing. sound becoming colour, colour sound. To sit outside the circle; to concentrate on the centre of the circle; to allow the music to draw earthly-mind into the man-dala. to be absorbed by the spinning centre, which would then cease to be the centre; cease to spin. To remain there at the centre of . . . IT . . . forever . . .

. . . A huge spinning wheel circling higher, enfolding, encom-passing, drawing him into the centre. Himself the dark axis of the wheel, the whole rotating faster & faster until it seemed to be perfectly still, but with colours flickering, emanating from him – the centre.

. . . He was surging thru space & downwards to earth. and the green & gold were part of him, stemmed from his body & spun outwards to form music with the air. with light. Wind carrying the wheel like a propeller out into the depths of the sky. & he was there with arms outstretched & mouth open as colours passed thru his shell body & re-entered as light. Round & round without moving. something ecstatic started to

tremble thru his body. thru the sound of wind & the sound of
colour & the music of colour he heard his own voice shouting.
Straining to hear his own words he felt sobs of joy shaking his
body, causing it to spin into revolutions of its own. the whirli-
gig of colour gyrating round his own small whirls. The voice
was shouting 'this is LIFE. love. life' the self circling ecstatic-
ally amid the larger throbbing circle of colour.

'Fear not the night's darkness'

Fear not the night's darkness
but see beyond it the rhythms
of shapes & colours
which echo back upon
the music of your thoughts.
Follow
into the exquisite world
where thoughts are born
of Silence.

Take the hand
which reaches so gently
from the reflection of water.
it is your own
leading you beyond your Self
into the region
where there is no Self or Other.

There linger
among the flowers
of Love and Peace.

Philip O'Connor

Poem on Self in form of events as modifiers of
self into thoughts to modify
the world to modify oneself

Prologue against Poetry

I ordered cornflakes by note from the grocer with sugar
and various other foods; I drove later to Portmadoc and
the traffic was considerable; I feared all the time as I have all my
    life
that I would be raped, which set me to thinking again,
as I have again and again, what this self that could be raped
consisted of; and what would result from rape,
and I strove to put into other, expansive words, words
leading to fuller concepts, the together meaning of this rape
as a fact. (Integrity is a word I cannot use – I always say
those who have it allow it to look after itself
and those who haven't worry about it all their lives,
for ever guarding it. One guards only the absent in oneself.)

Putting all this down now I ask me and you: Is this Poetry?
And I have to admit that if it is I do not know what is not,
And if it is not I do not know what is: briefly, I do not know
    poetry.

This whatever it may be called by professional callers,
a body among whom I am not to be numbered,
is in effect a search for, like indeed so many poems,
like perhaps the majority of poems to this point in history
(when the self remains unsalvaged from other selves
possibly because it is not separate from other selves

and our attempt to separate it
merely reflects our systematically organized
isolation) – is indeed a search for
whatever of self is, as they so deplorably (and advertisingly)
    say –
unique: I would not like to succeed in this quest. I would like
    to fail

in order to succeed in a greater quest: what are you, and be led
    to this
from the point wherein I fail to know what I am.

Is this in effect a prologue against poetry? No.
It is a prologue against what I have come to associate with
    poetry:
lies arranged by a dead form; dead forms make lies. Poetry as I
    have come
to think of it is a dead form.

Maybe this belongs to such a form: I don't know; I think
that I don't care.

I

My starting point in life was that I did not know differences,
and my intermediate point was that I failed to make connexions
    necessary
to my nourishment as soon as I saw differences that were
    alarming,
and my later development was an abstinence from definition
and an abstinence from that abstinence; briefly,
a hopeful dissolution of protective attitudes and mental stances.
I give myself every permission in thought looking never for
    consistency
and order and never seeking the lack of them.

My starting point in life was that I did not know differences
as 'vital' and to me as alarming
as those known, it seems and seemed to me, to my elders
and above all when the time came to my educators,
who appeared to me to be obsessed (hallucinated) by differences;
I can hear still the typewriter tap of the pedagogic voice
damning phenomena into their differences
and then sodomously allowing in a quaver of mystical defeat
certain 'wonderful' connexions.

My starting point in life was that I didn't know differences;
hence I gather that myself was mainly feeling of textures,
such as my mother's skin and textiles and objects,
all of which were solved into a common denominator,
which was I in my creche, my safety.

As I grew up and observed and noted such phenomena being
    sent from me
with names like masterful riders taking them across horizons I
    would never reach
and beyond which lay, may I say, the thunder of madness,
I developed an understandable sense of isolation;
for I must insist that phenomena and the skin of my mother
were similars, and I must know that she went with them, as she
    did.

So I in isolation was an early sensation and feeling,
and very soon an observation; there grew a wider ring around
    me,
and from me to the ring, to the frontier, lay grey emptiness
    whose
emptiness being vacuous might if I relaxed
suck transmogrified the departed things and a person.

So was determined the I I conceived, and I have not known
    another
and in, perhaps, an excessive simplicity, I have aspired to know
    another I,
which I think may not be: Know thyself is Know they self-
    conception,
a capitalistic measure of viable hallucination.

I must say that the skin of my mother and her voice
were sooner mine than her person, which I never knew,
and which I created therefore in replica from absence
to guard me when she did not.
I was my mother; how can I fit in those exiled phenomena with
    her?

I will leave them; they may return.

For I have omitted to write that beyond the horizon to which
exiled phenomena had been ridden away
by definitive riders in armour got from aliens
lay a more detailed world than I have expressed
as the thunder of madness, to which it was said I was slightly
    prone
by those who identified themselves with the aliens
in order to be safe: to whom they had been frightened as
    consorts.

I may say that beyond that frontier lay the cattle of knowledge
    so-called,
lay phenomena out of my context,
lay a rowdy bric-à-brac which it was heresy to attempt to
    understand,
because disconnexion and alienation was the faith of the people
from the ordinances of their masters who seemed to be people.

I may say that my lovers, my phenomena,
against which I had proned in the summertime of an infancy
    somewhat restless,
appeared to me quickly to be almost be-headed, to have had
    their brains
leucotomized,
to be deadened into the parlance of alien knowledge,
that they were quickly tortured to facts which fed knowledge
which was a machine constructed to mangle our true brains,
such true brains being ever the nestlers in our sweet bodies,
which love informs in life.

I saw that we the children were attached with facts
by educators who wished us to share
their own estrangement from such facts, which estrangement
    was created
by the murdering of phenomena into facts. For we were little
    Christs
tortured to give up the world, O Fools, to make of it thus
this sediment of reality, this sludge of existence
so known to you, poor reader.

At school I quavered to hear a fact announced,
I squirmed and sweated to see the approach of this surgical
    instrument
designed to cleave me in two; but my resistance to this cleavage
was later heralded as schizophrenia: which, dear reader,
is what schizophrenia is: the rebellion against such a division
into the sensuous, around which living mind is clotted,
and abstract fact, which sucks the elixir of life, distilled to
    spirit.

2

I made me a self to negotiate the grey vacuum vacated by
   phenomena
which would phantasmagorically return as facts
and by my mother who would phantasmagorically return as
   the women
who were not she when unveiled.
How to make a self? It is easy, too easy.
Take a pair of sparkling eyes –
take a pair of ruby lips –
take the woman who has gone away
and see her in the daily mirror of your life.

Take the gone one's voice's song
and whisper she is you –
augment, and amplify the portrait.
Cover it with molasses of tears unshed –
carve round it the antique warrior you never saw
(the father whose cosmetic is gore)
and you have a self prone to disintegration.

Strut and prance in the auditorium of your solitary observing
   self,
play to you, check it and improve it, give it your heart and
   soul
('he is self-centred' – thus the fools:
he is eccentred, thus I know)
live for it night and day, and find this retribution:
that the player steals the audience
and a dreadful quarrel ensues,
an equivocation lasting half a lifetime,
a quarrel as to who am I;
a tug of war
between wife and whore.

Retribution? Has an answer, as have all questions asked
to excess. Send with a withered secret grin of destructive
    anticipation
this fabricated player-self into the world – close the theatre
'go' into the world (It goes, not the audience you)
and watch it with delight
be smashed; grubbily stare the strewn parts
of the makeshift player and dare – dare at your peril then say:
the real I is the one who stares with glee
at the destruction of the foundered he:
for this is not so.

Once again I had no I; definition was felicitously removed
    again.
Now I wonder in the mist
by what creator I'll be kissed; and his name
is surely Everything.

Thus I learned by use of this proxy self
to disregard action until it anchored once again
into me.
I would not agitate, which was to speculate,
which speculation was operated
by the conjoint unharmonious pair
of the allegedly true I and the self-conception.

3
There endured a long time of no-self;
each presumer to the throne
was rejected; in the mirror the face slowly
wore out, and the mask like an empty cake tin
yawned its weary dissolution.

Rejecting all selves within my knowledge
I saw that most of us are in the same boat,
and I could not believe the you of you
equally with the I of I.

To be sundered from all conception of self
needs the prop of disbelieving in your conception of you,
which I saw the play with all the lifeless vivacity
of the I of I.

I took for then profound
the dictum of Shakespeare, sent to cliché by uncomprehending
    men –
that all the world is a stage: which I amend:
all this limited world.
For there's another outside the theatre,
in its animating context.

I lay like oil on water,
like milk on infant's lip,
moved by a satisfying unknown larger wave,
and I basked for many many years
under the sky, avoiding roofs.

One day I would be called to the core, I surmised,
and I became the pilgrim of the call, which silenced it.

Do not pursue what will inevitably come,
or flee what should arrive.

4

In those years I playfully made (avoiding the pundits' grimy
reach)
a theory of self, summarized in the words 'anything' and
'anyhow':
know not thyself, I presumptuously said,
and fell to bed in another definition (of anti-definition):
to point which I will quote:

'Not to regard knowing as knowing is the highest.*
To regard not-knowing as knowing is a sickness.
Indeed, it is only by being sick of that sickness one is not sick.
The Saint is not sick because he is sick of that sickness.
Therefore he is not sick.'

5

Later I strayed into the cult of the spontaneous,
which in these unguarded times wears an air of gamy spring-
time;
but this by eschewing made volition a demon exorcized in
madness;
voliton to be undermined must be contained;
volition and the spontaneous are a pair to go.

6

When I go to foreign places
and all with people are foreign
because such is this world in which we are made to each other
foreigners
I fear to be raped;
what is this fear, what is this I?

* Tao Te Ching

The rape is conversion by force into you;
the I is the weakness of it constructed in your despite.
As long, dear reader, as we are I against others,
constructs built in a relative difference,
we are prone to rape, to defence, to offence.

How shall I write the new I unborn?

A cliché must serve: as a flower in a garden,
as an individual in a community, whose sap
is everyone's, and the garden of them the world to be.

I can sustain no defence without sickness;
from which I know that we are alike,
from which I reject our patented differences.

True difference blooms without patents,
and its nourishment is commonness.
In a fit of early madness dreaming of the coalescence I sang that
    I am you;
I know better.
To be like you is nearer, because identity is annihilation –
identity thrown at me which makes me try to jump into yours –
fences are the curse of humanity.

So alien are we that only love, that exhausted concoction sweet
    though it be,
can place us within civilized calling distance.

Sometimes when I go to Portmadoc I think of shopping and
    my family.

Neil Oram

Heaven's Below

'Heaven's below
whilst Hell's up above,'
said a stranded fish
to a passing dove.

'No! Hell's in the water
and Heaven's out of reach,'
said the peaceful bird
to the fish on the beach.

A poetic cat
smiled in bliss,
believing the bird
was wooing the fish.

Said the bird to the fish
'There's our devil.'
The fish went white
and the bird went yellow.

The fish in a panic,
with one leap
reached the sea.
The dove cooed goodbye
and flew up to a tree.

Said the cat to himself,
'what heaven it would be,
to fly like a bird
and swim in the sea.'

Cross

'*The accuser is the devil. The spirit of Jesus Christ is eternal forgiveness of sin.*'   *W. Blake*

You want the high?	*O Lord Jesus Christ*
high hot?	
you want yak track?	*we lie in great darkness*
you want sash rash?	
you sash rash?	
sash rippling silk greed sea.	*straining to raise ourselves*
You sweat palm?	
foam fingers? mushroom?	
your room foaming?	*out of our corruption. O Lord*
marked without mask?	
You mask? Trussed scream?	
Can't trust trussed scream.	*save us from our vanity*
You screen? Vein from sky?	
you collapse under lie?	
you crinkle of grained glass?	*Wash our souls free*
you gramophone? collapsible lie?	
Transferable? lie for lie?	
You! Greed? rippling?	*of all images of you.*
you green sky sweating?	
you sweating under lie?	
you run from crack crinkle?	*A starling cries and I cry*
Fear mind bang? crack fear?	
You? mess under mind?	
Me lash you trash! smash	
mask!	LIFE O GOD O GRASP ME
O! you groan roam the	
moon, eh!	
You cry 'TRICKED, TRIED BY	
TRASH' EH!	

You collapse under mind! EH? *thaw me out of explanations*
'me strangled by blood,
maimed song of the sky
not veins of light   *and fill our hearts with simple*
            warmth.

vain scaffold of right
grime rust of the mind
smashed forehead of night   *Only your unsentimental*
           love

sight smeared with mesh.
I'm mashed in your mesh,
I'm mashed in your mesh'   *can dissolve our selfishness*
I'll mash you trash
I've tracked you tower
we slaughter borders   *and save us* LORD
you papered with birds.
Does your cashflesh flash?
I've TRACKED YOU TRASH! *from strange powers and*
          mysteries.

O LORD DESTROY THIS MESH WHICH TRIES TO MASH
  THE WORD

Bright High Lay

It is autumn in the garden. The leaves are falling. My hand
grows old. My heart is wind-swept snow. O!!! I enter. Alone.
Listen . . . snow falling? I am here again. Listen . . . singing? It
is always beginning. The wound of awakening dissolves in the
violet kiss of eternity. The clouds are far below, all is still within
the flower. What is night like from above? Lying in a jewel of
light. The stars are fierce. The earth is listening to the endless
dancing snow. The earth dissolves in the listening. The snow is

light. The perfume heart. The celestial ache. The burning
liquid-fire, called flesh, is the loom. The only thread is love, is
love.

No Stile

One night, a poem found me
placing everything where it belongs;
gently showed me the LIVING TRUTH
that's veiled by literature.
It came upon me singing, flowering
from the flow, not built up
by strain. Sunlight melting
the glacier of my effort. grace. everything
is alive.

Imprisonment is a conviction.
This poem prevents comparison.
It found me when I was walking by the river
an autumn evening   after the rain
everything, a humming burning stillness.
It kicked out all sentiment
dumbness replaced the drumming brain.
In the shock I almost froze.
We ARE and all IS.
leaves on your shoes
falling on cars
the freezing shock . . . where we are
is not a passing through;
but where we are, is where we pass to.
That corner which you pass by,
that familiar crossroad holds the sky
of infinity, which you must drown in.

Stand still there, as cars pass by,
and SEE, before you see
the willow-latticed-sky;
but isn't this the moment which you fear,
your crumpled heart
unfolding in your heart?

Straight

A way of life. To paint
when all is still.
The quiet morning stirs
the cold light
slowly kills
the stars. The patio
vaguely mirrors
clouds.
aroma . . . .
caressed by the sounds
of shifting leaves.

To live the life of thankfulness. This house
with white walls in and out,
where dogma's plans dissolve in love
of life. Where morning light will thrill my heart
to prayer. My hands feel warm in the sound
of the distant sea.
To have a wife
whose soul beams beauty,
whose quiet feet
delight upon the cold slab
in the shimmering morning light,
her white dress chuckling
in the breeze.

'Do not seek...'

Do not seek
for gentleness it comes
as gentle as the moon
floats
through the day
as gentle as these white
flowers on my palm
flickering
in a sunless
rain-near
breeze

Lament

O frenzied fingers grappling to hook
the earth's heart, be still. O white hills
and still starlight do I grieve alone? Am I cactus
abandoned on the reptile tongue? No songs
I sing could breach this gaping jaw. Only stillness
can be sung. Who can dare
to stand alone
in this ever moving downward falling doom we chose?
O what have we done?

Who can listen amidst the clatter to the stillness
of the star called the HEART, and not run, knowing
all seeking is decay? Who can stand still
in this crater of the ripped throat, and not accuse?
O I stand in awe in this paradise of the open heart
and see that every answer is a grave. O the scarecrow
points the way. With arms outstretched

he pirouettes: a whirling cross. O listen love
is stillness, an endless forgiveness. Do not run
from this burning sea into the freezing
dazed desert of the threadbare heart. O cry!
Cry! Cry! O precious oasis of tears. The morning throbs
in every flower then collides, slain
upon the altar of the brain. O father! Shadows
bought your soul with words, but I also followed
the moon, the moon crumbling into a snake. O Hills
give me the strength of your still light to look
into her sacred heart, as she spits
poison in my eyes. O Hills, these waves
called fear, are love.

Tilled Lie

Though I speak with the tongues of men
　　　　　　'your IDEA of truth . . . is fantasy' – EDDIE

Soaked with hush
the Palace breathes,
from listening trees fall frozen leaves.
The still air trembles
the stars unfold . . . an endless opening crystal bowl.

and of angels and have not charity,

Ghosts like snow, fall through my breast;
but unafraid I stretch straight through . . . .
from detail . . . wing-ripped . . . crawl to you
a clock-work wilderness of who.

I am become as sounding brass or a tinkling cymbal.

Yet I have ringed her wrists of snow
sculptured   film-still   quiet   bone
can't we together grow alone?

And though I have all faith, so that I could

Seeing this way
now like that,
everything changing
as bright as a flash.
Listening in awe
the colours grow,
saw green-lit grottos
inside my bones.
Like a tent
made of glass
or an upturned boat,
the night has a structure
which love unfolds.

remove mountains, and have not charity,

All this you know, and yet you fear the break
ripping the pulsing lace-light in your haste,
racing away from me and all you've sown,
searching to find a reason not to grow.
All this you know . . . .

I am nothing.

1 Corinthians 13

Stale Lay

The middle-man is an image
not a man.
It is your fear of flying
ln the fire.

Change the charge
the iron filings fly,
a mass belief in death
will fade from view.
Many say that words are never true,
referring to misuse
they fade from view.
The miracle not seen
they rave of highs,
the startling shock
is seeing that we are.

The middle-man is a process
which you choose,
instead of looking through
to what is there.
Authority without your thought
would stare,
referring to the past
is how it rapes.

The middle-man is hungry for your core
his reel of rules within you
teach escape;
the fear of travelling past them
holds your core,
the moon within the sea
eats up the shape.

Sly Strain

Awkward shouts, came more silently than audibly from the
distant salt dunes. Are they all frozen there in the hot sun?

Lovers, erased by the harsh winds, sculptures decayed into mounds. Can only dogs inhabit this petrified landscape?

Suddenly she walks beneath green trees created from her intoxicating love. All manner of soft animals jump and skip about her, as she slowly walks through this garden of Heaven.

Does she care that she will find no one there at the edge of the lake?

Nothing stirs her fear.

The lake is of course her heart, dancing in the clear ringing air. Butterflies. Flowers swaying. She sits quietly by the water's edge, embraced by the sparkling dance of light.

The moment is pure music.

Soon, she walks back through the woods, and every creature, tree, grass and flower, thank her, knowing they will be forever nourished by her vision of love.

Still Storm

Now that he is gone
books
mean nothing, instead
the ordinary day
swirls so strangely . . .

Overwhelming emptiness
meets the sunlit room.

Where there was words and waiting
for response, becomes the sound
of my silence, shattered continuously
by speculation, my breathing and
our child.

In his absence natural pain
returns, bringing with it joy
in my own growth, the nakedness,
which, seeking for it, clothes.

What does he do in rooms alone like this?
Does he sit burnt by the gentle frenzy
of the flowers, does he let his ache have room
to pulse, does he cherish subtility and place
his utter heart within it, or does he? . . .

Tom Pickard

The Work

writing poems
(keeping rabbits)
each day the shite
to be cleared
fresh straw to be laid

High on the Walls

strange to be higher
than a bird, to watch
them eat

when startled (the only
defence to be above)
take flight, and land
at my feet

The Street Cleaner with his
Eighteenth Century Muck Cart

must have been used for 'bring out your dead'
giant mexican-hat wheels, no handles,
to be pushed along after the brush has done its job

and the wheels make the same sounds on the cobbles,
an employee at the corporation yard, but smiles,
a flat cap, a boiler suit, but still that look
                    of the eighteenth century

you would say an idiot smile though I say old turnips and blobs
in his cart with straw and broken glass are typical.
He is his own man.

For: Franky and Grailly And Tweddle and Mel in a Pub or in a cell

Av got the horny* blues, av got the horny blues
if your gonna be naughty, ya gonna get the horny blues.

When you see the meat waggin you got t stop shaggin
If your doin some screwin, they'l be there whistles blowin
you get the horny blues, you got the horny blues
if your gonna be naughty your gonna get the hornys after you

Smokin of the herb, drinkin of the wine
your sure t be disturbed by PC 49
youve got the horny blues, the horny blues
if your gonna be naughty your gonna get the hornys chainin
    you

Start up a barny, they'l bring in an army
but kick one in the teeth, it'l make you feel so sweet,
you get the horny blues, you get the horny blues
if your gonna be naughty your gonna get the horny blues

* horny=police

They'l take you to the cell, black in your eye
satisfy those hornys too, those hornys too
if your gonna be naughty
ya gonna get the horny blues.

The Daylight Hours
Song for Dole Wallas

A hev gorra bairn
an a hev gorra wife
an a cannit see me bairn or wife
workin in the night,

So go way Mr Doleman
av got somethin else ti do
than spen me daylight hours
workin for you.

Yes aa am a song bird
an a song bird must sing
an you, oh Mr Doleman
you'll not clip me wings.

So go way Mr Doleman
av got somethin else ti do
than spen me daylight hours
workin for you.

Grab ya job an ram it
in ya stupid gob
ad ratha gan ti prison
than de ya stinkin job.

So go way Mr Doleman
av got somethin else ti do
than spen me daylight hours
workin for you.

An if a gan ti prison
the world will git ti na
the walls of a prison
isin strang enuff for wa.

So grab ya job an ram it
in ya stupid gob
ad rather gan ti prison
than de ya stinkin job.

Hunga

Theres a pain in my stomach called hunga
it happens six days of the week
on friday wi gan t'the assistance
thi give us some money to seek
and to see some way of payin wa way
some way of payin wa way
fora day
some way of payin wa way.

On monday wi gan wi oot bacon
on tuesday wi gan wi oot meat
on wensday wi gan wi oot bread
on thursday wi gits nowt ti eet
on friday aa gans an aa begs

Theres a pain in my stomach called hunga
it happens six days of the week
on friday wi gan ti the assistance
thi give us some money to seek
and to see some way of payin wa way
some way of payin wa way
fora day
some way of payin wa way.

    Av not got the money ti buy her new clothes
    av not got the money ti buy him some toys
    al not git me hair cut
    al not git a job
    ad rather be skint than an industrial cog.

Theres a pain in my stomach called hunga
it happens six days of the week
on friday aa gans ti the assistance
they give us some money to seek
and to see some way of payin wa way
some way of payin wa way
fora day
some way of payin wa way.

    Thi send a inspecta roond
    each day of the week
    ti see if am lookin for work,
    but av got me coat on
    an walkin the toon
    forst tryin to borro a short.

Theres a pain in my stomach called hunga
it happens six days of the week

on friday a gan ti the assistance
they give us some money to seek
and to see some way of payin wa way
some way of payin wa way
fora day
some way of payin wa way.

Shag

canny bord ower there
sharrap man yi think i nowt but tarts

divin na though
wouden mind a bash arrit

hoo pet can a tek yi yem?
am a big streng lad
al luk after yi

a na ya not owld inuff ti suck a dummy

hoo lads tommys scored
whats ya name pet
howear gis a kiss
gis a bit feel pet
di yi fancy a meat injectin?
well jump on the end i this

suck me plums
gis a suck off

o yi commin fora walk wis?
will gan ower the quarry
a nas a shortcut

leave is alen

sharrap or al belt yi

grab a
gis a bit feel
pull a doon
lets have a bit tit
howear man am forst

am warnin yis al git the coppas

sharrap or al kick ya teeth in

pull a doon
rip a skort off
hurry up an stuff it tom
its me next

are man quick
stick it in the get
howld a doon
shi winnit keep still
well hit the twat
please keep still pet an a winnit be a minit
go on man go on
a-a-r-r-r thatsnice

howear well
its me next.

Scrap

hoo kids
fancy yasel?

aye
howear ootside

scrap lads, whos jumpin in?

kick ees heed in
gerroot yi twat
stick it on im
kick ees pills
boorim in the nackers man
wipe ees face wi ya raza
smash the get

are nar thats noron
sharrap oral kill yi

twat

fluffy bum
puff
shite hawk

suck ees plums
boot im one
bottle im

heres a horny
the black enameld hoer

scarper lads

Paul Potts

From 'Dante called you Beatrice'

I want to write something holy
Holy about life
Where a kiss is a prayer
And God is worshipped
By the way a woman combs her hair.

. . . When I saw a lark fly through the air, I thought of a rainbow playing on your hair. For you walk the way an angel plays a lyre.

When boys and girls go out to play there is always someone left behind, and the boy who is left behind is no use to the girl who is left behind.

If I wrote the greatest love song since that young Judaean King took down his harp to fill Jerusalem's air, she could not hear. Yet if I had a lot of sex appeal, she would have thought my lies more beautiful than the flowers I brought her, grown from seeds found in a Hebrew barn.

My thoughts have taken your thoughts in their arms. My need has kissed your loneliness on the brow. Eve and morrow, fast and festival. My heart has waited on the going of your sorrow.

. . . Sometimes my love makes me snow blind. So, as the burnished sun curves upwards in the sky through all the whiteness of an arctic day, and a long dead winter is miracled to spring, I see moving towards me the shadow of a woman and the shadow of a child.

The beauty of a woman's body can make the beauty in a man's mind become more beautiful still. My heart is her lover, my spirit her spouse. My dreams are her children: she brings them up well. My mind is more beautiful than ever it could have been if I had not seen her body. My spirit has kissed her, my soul has held her in its arms.

Once I saw my thoughts drive the sorrow from her face, that was the nearest I got to a vision beheld.

And now I am alone again, alone with my dream. And this is my dream. That one day here on this earth, everybody who is born will live out their life to its just end, in love, reverence, excitement and happiness. How this is going to happen I don't know. That it just might possibly really happen, I believe is worth believing. Now should they be tempted to laugh at my dream, I must warn them, that their laughter will only be heard as an echo against the walls of that dream.

Horseman, ride on, past a world of motor-scooters and suburbs where there is no hay for your horse and no sword for your foes. Because if I had won fame, I would have used it, in defence of humble things and in the service of the rare.

Tom Raworth

You Were Wearing Blue

the explosions are nearer this evening
the last train leaves for the south
at six   tomorrow
the announcements will be in a different language

i chew the end of a match
the tips of my finger and thumb are sticky

i will wait at the station & you
will send a note, i will
read it
        it will be raining

        our shadows in the electric light

when i was eight they taught me *real*
writing
        to join up the letters

listen you said i
preferred to look
        at the sea.   everything stops there at strange angles

only the boats spoil it
making you focus further

My Face Is My Own, I Thought

morning   he had gone
down to the village   a figure
she still recognized from his walk

nothing
          he had explained
is won by arguing   things are changed
only by power
                  and cunning   she still sat
meaning to ask what
did you say   ?   echo in her ears

he might just have finished speaking   so
waiting and
              taking the scissors
began to trim off the baby's fingers

Wedding Day

noise of a ring sliding onto a finger

supposing he *did* say that?
we came by the front
sea fog twisting light above the pebbles
towards the cliffs towards the sea

i made this pact, intelligence
shall not replace intuition, sitting here
my hand cold on the typewriter
flicking the corner of the paper.   he

came from the toilet wearing
a suit, people
didn't recognize him, down the length of
corridor.   the room
was wooden, sunlight   we stood in a half circle

noise of two cine-cameras

i wonder what's wrong with her
face, she said, because
there's nothing wrong with it really   i
inhabit a place just to the left of that phrase.   from

a bath the father took champagne later
whiskey.   through the window we watched the frigate's
orange raft drifting to shore

i mean if you're taking *that*
attitude
            we rode in a train watching the dog move

noise of a bicycle freewheeling downhill

'but i don' *love*'

but i don' *love*
you she said   there were
drops of sweat
                  on the receiver
warm sun the sky
on the horizon turquoise   a faint
haze
        red trains crossed the bridge

they played war forecast music   as they
walked down the hill the brown
girls passed
                    driving their own cars

the tree had not been climbed they
disturbed the dirt   it grew
like a ladder
from below the sound of water on the leaves

but she said you stroked her
hair she said she is like a
cow you are so
obvious

the gardens of the houses go down
to the stream   there are a few
allotments the path
was overgrown   they walked single file
under the north circular road   the tunnel
chalk inscriptions latest dated 1958
                                    no sound
from the cars overhead
                        the lake
dark red flowers   green
scum no
current a red
ball
      stationary in the middle

Morning

she came in laughing his
shit's blue and red today those
wax crayons he ate last night   you know
he said eating the cake the
first thing nurses learn
is how to get rid of an erection say
you get one whilst they're shaving
you, they give it a knock like
this, he flicked his hand and
waved it down she
screamed, the baby stood in the doorway
carrying the cat
in the cat's mouth a bird fluttered

Sky
(*for Ron Padgett*)

of the burned building but the frame stays
my room was there, stopping the clouds from entering
and i was inside. i opened a window – sky!
a skylight – blue again! a trapdoor in the floor
saw the roof of an airplane passing under me

i somersaulted slowly in that room, not touching anything
blind almonds falling

Going Away Poem for Lee Harwood

the woodsmoke hangs in the air between the trees
click – it is winter, the smoke vanishes

and now the orange flames provide a movement
across the water – it is the children
pay for it   their faulty articulation
not really jerks, but a slowness of legs and larynx

seen in the flashes of blue light from the train wheels
as we are travelling, separated from the crude metal
by point 008 of an inch of candlewax
left by the spraying machines that only run at night

                                                        fever

asleep in a beached boat, covered with foreign newspapers
in a city on a bay where even the light is different
as the deprived are always the state of the nation

The Empty Pain-Killer Bottles

bite, and the taste of tongues
slimy. drinking spit
she dribbled.

the photographs and secret letters
have melted my wallet, are growing into me
the centipedes are in my veins, swimming against the tide

would i eat her snot under that warm protection?
sure. and listen without laughing
to her tales of mice in the sleeve of that old dress

cheese from her body packed in sandalwood
a pickled finger she gave me as a keepsake
annabella, such a ridiculous name for a breakfast cereal

Collapsible

behind the calm famous faces knowledge of what crimes?
rain on one window showing the wind's direction

a jackdaw collecting phrases   'it's a chicken!'
nothing lonelier than hearing your own pop in another country

               whose face with bandages was singing
her breath always only half an inch from the corner of my eye

Variations

do you remember a hill, miranda?
and the times we'd sit on the cool veranda
talking of films, was it bande a
part from you there is no one miranda
and just about here i had planned to
change the rhyme
just one more time
a reverse.   last line

miranda.   a hill.   i remember.   do you?

Hot Day at the Races

in the bramble bush shelley slowly eats a lark's heart
we've had quite a bit of rain since you were here last
raw silk goes on soft ground (result of looking in the form
    book)
two foggy dell seven to two three ran
crouched, the blood drips on his knees
and horses pass

shelley knows where the rails end
did i tell you about the blinkered runners?

shelley is waiting with a cross-bow for his rival, the jockey
all day he's watched the races from his bush
now, with eight and a half furlongs to go
raw silk at least four lengths back disputing third place
he takes aim

and horses pass

his rival, the jockey, soars in the air
and falls.   the lark's beak neatly pierces his eye

Carlyle Reedy

O the monumental dignity of the cow

O the monumental dignity of the cow
                                                    the wind
does not even startle   her hair

Have you noted the white areas

Have you noted the white areas
of the cows disappearing as snow
clouds   gather   behind them

Bernard Saint

'What I am'

What I am
a white chalk man between chalk walls.

Where is the pulse that linked my blood to flowers?
Where, my white children?
Pale from your cold beds of pale sheets I see
you have lost the lusty
copra sinew, the hard copper jaw
the rhythm in your stiffened loins has lost its ecstasy.

Sad man with befloured face and buttered hair
your smeared grin mocks the gentle alchemy of Nature
You desecrate the hillside with pylons,
the body with clothes
What right have you to bring flowers
to the graves of your blossoming dead?

I will walk your metallic hills no more
Nor tread your asphalt plains.
I would hear the forgotten drums echo out
from lost savannahs,
remember the noonday heat on a naked thigh.

When I hear the rhythm in the wings of cranes
or the highproud jazz of Parker or Coltrane
rear up above rooftops
The pallor of my soul turns into shadow
My blood like molten bronze pounds deep in my chalk skull
the dark poetry of the basic man
moulds my molten thoughts.

In your church services
The tense atmosphere of the musty air
reminds me of the voodoo rite before the drums begin.
Crow of Cock! Blood of Goat! and the drumming
of bare feet on sand

I am sacrificed in these harsh steel corridors
to the white man's god
of cities and despair.

Michael Shayer

reading the *Observer* and absorbing its high tone

It's alright, you bastards,
    when some Russian
        or a New York Jew
shouts out in poetry
    then you think, it's   colourful
    you even print translations (poor ones)
    in your bloody papers
when it suits your book
to sneer
    at transatlantic barbarians
    unknowingly giving
    the American show away
or at the Russian at the one time
    making the rebel-act
    shaking down his Commissars
    and writing bad poems
which you can, still at the same
and bloody one same time
    get a kick from
    pretending as if you would ever
    have that same courage
while of course having
    it quite clear
    that it's not poetry
    doesn't have the basic craft
– not, this is, if written first
in English
    it wouldn't have had

but with these foreigners
      there's no need to apply
the same high rigorous standards
    by which you keep
        such impertinent poseurs
from ever ever ever ever ever
jazzing Shakespere's language
Where's your balls – or were you even born that way?

David Sladen

At the Dun Laoghaire Bus Terminus

At the Dun Laoghaire bus terminus there isn't space to turn:
The buses come in backwards, brake, rev, and conk out for
    five minutes.
Top deck, cheek pressed to window,
I watch one sliding in beside me, close as inches.

Not for the first time I see, moving behind the bus,
The little man waving his arms at the bus,
Playing the bus, almost, into its berth.

By the time the bus finally brakes, revs, and conks out,
The man has gone: I picture him
Under the chassis, proof that he has guided straight.

Oh we all try and help each other.

The truth is something else, not for the first time.
The truth is the busdrivers pay absolutely no mind to
The little man, who operates purely for his own benefit:
His signs are erratic, he's somewhat spastic; and if you want
    more,
The truth is he's deaf and dumb.

So tolerant are these people however,
That they permit the little man to stand behind the buses
And direct them in.
Since they can't ask him, no doubt they have to believe it,
That this makes him happy.

At home we'd be worried, and have him away and locked up,
Lest he fell underneath.
In the Dun Laoghaire bus terminus however, they respect
The element of risk.

And I watch from the window saying to myself,
It can't go on, it can't go on!

Tom Taylor

High Sequence

Sometimes I
      feel
  like I have a hole
    through my
  head which goes through
     my body
   and right through the
      earth on which I walk

Suddenly! as I walk along the road
   flash past two oil tankers
    one after the other
     and cars and buses
  and I can tell which of them are empty
    by the way they bounce
     on the road

   Sitting listening to Indian
        music
I realize I just gotta have this music
   I gotta have it for my breakfast
    but I can't

  High again

I feel like I am surrounded
    by a blanket
   No I don't –

This is what I feel like
        I feel like just
sitting and staring and
                listening to the music
pounding from the box
    the thundering box –

    I sit
            I feel my words tied
                        together
        by pieces of rope
                inarticulate sounds
                but they are clear
                I make –
                I hear the noises
                    from the source of supply
            from the
            musty cloudy sky blue
        sky   blue sky
            Violence is a drag
                it brings me down
                    people speaking bring me down
        but I dig the great noise
            of the people
            booming   booming
                                erratic noise

            I am inert
            I am powerful
    my mind is in control of myself

            Sitting on a crosslegged moonbeam
                speaking and blowing
                    puffs of gunsmoke
                    to the joy
                            of the full moon

when I am surrounded
      by people in white coats
   who chain me and
  leave me hanging from the
       bottom of the earth   ...

The Roses

There was a man
     with a hole in his head
        a big hole
    with no hair
   where the roses grew

Barry Tebb

School Smell

Composed of chalk dust,
Pencilshavings and
The sharp odour
Of stale urine;
It meets me now and then
Creeping down a creosoted corridor
Or waiting to be banged
With the dust from piles of books
On top of a cupboard.

The double desks heeled with iron
Have long been replaced;
The steel nibbed pens and
Ink watered to pale grey
Gone too: the cane's bamboo bite
Has nothing left to bite on
And David's psalms
Must learn each other.

But its there
Ready to spring out
Like a coiled snake skin still envenomed
After years by a suburban hearth.

It was fifteen years ago
But I still remember Smigger,
Our greying old headmaster
In his spats and striped trousers,

The last in our town to wear them,
And his northern accent,
Heavy as Sunday.
'Now then you lads,
I'm not having this
Or I'll tan you all,'
He'd bawl at a mill-hand's boy
For drawing cunts on the lavatory wall.

Old Holmes, too, his yellow teeth
And hair all over the place,
One hand trembling with shell shock,
The other with rage, one foot lame
And brain half-daft,
Ready to belt you
For moving an eye.

The boys were always
Belching and farting
And tormenting me for my
Long words and soft voice;
And they do still
When I sense that stink
In my nostrils.

Chris Torrance

South London Prose Poem

Sunset over a waste of allotments tended by gnomes: rows of squat houses with lazily smoking chimneys. Small gnomish houses surrounded by a waste of decaying allotments tended by dwarfish men smoking pipes.

Rows of painted brick houses and untidy back gardens, cabbage plots and patches of weedstrewn earth narrowly bisected by wandering muddy paths. A slow dreamy sunset curling away over the dark rooves of dwarfish little houses inhabited by gnomes tending their decaying allotments.

Cabbage patches and small fields of earth and stones divided by scrubby hedgerows and pipesmoking gnomes carefully tending their unkempt gardens. The magnificent red sunset curling diaphanously into the heavens over a blue haze rising from the smoking bonfires and smoking chimneys of a smallish gnomish people meticulously tending to their weedstrewn allotments. Red clouds unfolding over fields of bare earth and row upon row of forlorn cabbage plants tenderly weeded by pipesmoking thoughtful gnomes. Need I say more. Need I say more? Have I missed anything?

O yes and I sit in my smallish gnomish room with Westerly view sketching out over the rooftops the curling diaphanous clouds of the sunset folding on to the dark rooves of a beetle-browed smallish gnomish people carefully cultivating their smallholdings of lonely cabbage plants and bare areas of weedy, unkempt earth.

Seven Winter Haiku

two old beggars sit
     with their pipes by a warm fire
cracking their toes

*

the gay thrush in the tree:
     the song of my rake
amongst the wet leaves

*

this bare tree touches
     me slightly with its sadness:
so far from summer!

*

while the leaves fall so
     from the trees, Basho's spirit
lives on in me

*

so cold tonight – not
     one single rice grain for the
Buddha!

*

the sandal maker working
     in the dark
has forgotten Buddha long ago

*

the furious cat
     mews piteously for food
two drunk old men!

green orange purple red
(*for vjc*)

we are together smoke
        from our eyes hangs
below the ceiling fingers

tender vagrant love
        like a blind man
essaying a light step along a city street

warm hooks of desire
                                implant
to pattern your body with the

energy of spectrums. and the Arctic
                melts. and seas
foam. open skylines to the heart! the

vaulted movements of love! &
                                breaking: we
circle and land, exhausted thankful warm glad

elate hungry
                and the poem
lies in wait
                for redemption
a tangle of lines.

an address to the soul

spending an afternoon listening to music
even tho infected by this music I can only

revel in its density, the shapes of its sounds
streamers of dark smoke blowing in an incandescent wind
because I am in search of pain

that it should come to this
these voices, this music, that smoke

I am seeking
a new, raw edge
your bowed head
reflects doubt in the faceless seizure
that follows the death
of some risqué entertainer
throwing himself from a tall building
to the pavement at a late, quiet hour

                              you
are shouting from a far-distant
place, the tip of an iceberg, a secret tent
I fall helplessly on to the knifeblade again
the messages skid across your black skull
burrowing in the glass cities of your fantasies
the faint glimmering in a blank wall
that never knew voice

perception   beauty
shatter against that
                    purblind wall,
that it should come to this

the drifting of incense smoke in a long hour
                              I keep my
own company for a moment, before
manning a machine-gun that,
in brief bursts, leaks
oil before dawn

but no amount of persuasion will move you
not even the stink of blood
that accompanies this poem to its
grave

Alexander Trocchi

The Man and the Moon

The night tinkles
a chromium cash register
the little balls are orderly in their slots
cats laugh, their pointed teeth
the Sisters of Mercy furl their nets

Who can penetrate his own midnight?
Curb the insectal sputter of his own silences
while that great yellow gob, the moon
a jaundiced eye
shouts up at his shanks from the wet streets?

Myrtle with the Light Blue Hair

I was like she was, hot, see?
a fat, lovable little boy
with an eye that peeped at her, what she
showed the toad,   & not coy . . .

the slicks, flats, elastic tensions
of her great,   her imperial thighs,
the torque of her hot delta which
smoked a 'turkish cigarette'
fr   me to see that she
was all lips & hips
at the green pod she burgeoned
downwards from like a butter bean.

Then, her belly dangling
like an egg on poach
she scissored her legs cleverlie
& spat out the roach
which I raised to my lips . . .

I was like she was and she at her ease
& ripe was she
as a thumbpress on a Camembert cheese
her chevron winey-dark like good game
as she came on me
& retrieved her cigarette which
like a flutist
she laid at her lip, inhaled
& threw it away b4
collecting me to her like a windy skirt
she leaned against me,   like a sea . . .

He Tasted History with a Yellow Tooth

The long tusktooth of his nether jaw
cast a yellow shadow
broke through the thin bone of history
loosing tides.
'My personal Ides,'
he said, wrote at night
red ink on cheap paper
his big quick letters (always for the greater glory of God)
round as nuts or girlbreasts
a terrible child's message to a world at war.

Eggs again.
My aunt laid an egg once, all smooth and creamy
you wanted to stroke it as you want to stroke a woman
but she was ashamed of it
and took it away from me.
I think she buried it in the garden –
anyway, there's a patch of violets there
ten yards from the stair
that goes to the loft where my uncle kept the saddles
and they bleed each spring,
in spring there is a bleeding.

He's a bit of a Jesuit
his brain full of bits of history
which he chews over with his yellow tooth,
a strange Balkan name, an Icelandic God,
Did you know that somewhere in Africa
a woman walks naked to her wedding?

I tell you there is no use talking about the 'Renaissance'
it was a falling off, a *ruining*
of towers (you know the derivation?)
Late? I suppose it is. Not want tea?
– I wonder when a woman will walk naked to me?

£   S   D
(love, sex, death
pounds, shillings, pence
lysergic acid)

Iron leaves glint,
where wind broke in,

red rot in rain:
my death is lead,
cloven by slow,
radium-sharp shark-fin.

In my soft tree-bole
bleeds pearl,
spreads spoor
of wee, unhungering,
ceaseless vole.

An end to blue and green
and tune;
no more delight
in the black cave
of yr feminine night:

the poor silt of my years
is thin to spread . . .
after I am dead, 'Margarine,'
it will be said,
'he mistook it for butter.'

An end to sun,
moon, sky,
no young girl now will lie
in hot halter
of a pregnancy.

. . . young witches,
old bitches,
silvered resilience
of stagelit thighs,
hot, husky cries,

mascaraed eyes,
all manner of highs,
excruciatingly artificial.

Few virtues,
threadbare ascription . . .
clues: blues
      cruise
      unpaid dues;
. . . dropped Plato
like a hot potato;
wouldn't work:
hashish of the Turk . . .

There was a door between
him and himself.
Out, like the biff-ball
from the bat,
the limit taut,
feet sunk in cement,
tripped over himself,
a closing hinge:
himself something
upon which he couldn't impinge.

Gael Turnbull

Thanks

Thanks, and praise for
the knot in the wood

across the grain
making the carpenter curse

where a branch sprang out
carrying sap to each leaf.

Now That April's Here

It's raining on the brussels sprouts.
The fire is smoking in the grate.
Jo Grimond says he has no doubts.
Will Oxford beat the Cambridge eight?

Some bright intervals tomorrow.
Sixpence on a football pool.
Seven percent if you want to borrow.
Charles is settling down at school.

Put the Great back in Great Britain.
Write a letter to *The Times*.
Lots of fun with Billy Butlin.
It's a poem if it rhymes.

An Irish Monk, on Lindisfarne, about 650 A.D.

A hesitation of the tide
betrays this island, daily.

On Iona, at dusk
(ago, how long ago?)
often (did it happen?)
I saw the Lord walking
in the surf amidst the gulls,
calling, 'Come. Have joy in Me.'

Yes, with these eyes.

Now, on strange rocks
(faintly through the wall)
echoing, the same sea roars.

Detail is my toil.
In chapel, verse by verse –
in the kitchen, loaf by loaf –
with my pen, word by word –

by imitation,
illumination.

The patience of the bricklayer
is assumed in the dream of the architect.

*

On the road coming, five days travel, a Pict woman (big mouth and small bones) gave me shelter, and laughed (part scorn, part pity) at my journey. 'What do you hope for, even if you get there, that you couldn't have had twice over in Ireland?'

Then I told her of the darkness amongst the barbarians and of the great light in the monasteries at home, and she replied, 'Will they thank you for that, you so young and naïve, and why should you go, you out of so many?'

I said that I heard a voice calling, and she said, 'So men dream, are unsatisfied, wear their legs out with walking, and you scarcely a boy out of school.'

So she laughed, and I leaned my head on my hands, feeling the thickness of dust in each palm.

Then she told me there was not another of her face left in that valley, not one, nothing left. 'And all in three generations. Once even Rome feared us. Now my children are mongrels. And my husband has left me. No matter. Or great matter. I am still a Pict.'

Then she fed me, put herbs on my feet, wished me well, and I blessed her but she said, 'Save that for yourself, you will need it, when your heart turns rancid, and your joints begin to stiffen on the foreign roads. Remember me, when you come, returning.'

So she mocked; and sometimes, even now, ten years later, I hear it as I waken (receding in a dream), that laughter, broad, without malice.

*

Returning,
in the mind, still there,
home:
– devout green hills
– intimate peat smoke
– a cow-bell beseeching
– warm fleece in my bed
– fresh water, fresh, a brook

Here:
– rain clouds like beggars' rags
– stench of burned weed
– fret of the chain-mail sea
– hard knees on cold stone
– dry saliva, salt fish

The gulls cry:
– believe
– achieve

The bells reply:
– some
– some

At the lowest ebb
you can leave dryshod
this fitful island.

The Scratching Sound

The scratching sound, in case you ask, comes from my finger
    nails working at a small crevice which I've discovered in
    the plaster,

beyond which, you don't have to tell me, there are probably
    bricks and even concrete,

and certainly most of my time is taken up with routine or even
    compulsory activities, which is just as well since my finger
    nails would never stand up to it for long at a time,

and admittedly there is an element of deliberate eccentricity
    since the scratching has a bizarre effect upon many of my
    companions, which does help to pass the time –

none-the-less, this particular crevice is far from exhausted; and,
    finally, I can see no other way out.

For Nicholas De Stael, his painting: 'Les Toits'

You have hidden it, that, there under the paint,
a colour, the subject of your picture,
which is there, somewhere,
under the tiles, slates, casements, chimney-pots:
that, whatever it is,
which you don't dare (you don't want)
to see any more,
a colour you once saw
which may still be there, which must be
there under the greys, greengreys, bluegreys, rainbowgreys:
that
colour of a knife, implacable colour, one colour
which you have covered up, pretending to paint a picture
of roof-tops –
to declare with such astonishing candour
what you could not conceal otherwise.

Thoughts on the 183rd birthday of J. M. W. Turner

A charge was inserted under the foundations and detonated . . .

The sun has disappeared leaving part of itself adherent to several fragments of vapour. A gold sovereign comes in handy as a replacement.

The sky has been pried loose from the horizon. The blue has taken the strain by splitting into radial fissures of indigo. Tack it together somehow with rivets of carmine.

Then go home, have a glass of sherry, and look at it again.

Tomorrow will begin the reconstruction of heaven. Meanwhile, this evening, demolition has its attractions.

Accidents, too, can be very useful.

Not to forget the weather. A very proper subject for conversation. The damp has penetrated more deeply than we might have supposed. The light itself is warped. Even the clouds are affected by mildew.

Our text for the occasion being: '. . . to preach deliverance to the captives and the recovery of sight to the blind, to set at liberty them that are bruised . . .'

The colours imprisoned in daylight.

The Priests of Paris

The priests in Paris are the priests of Paris.
The black ones, striding along the pavements, always
        striding somewhere, always purposefully going,
some with hats like platters, some in skull caps, some
        with shaven pates,
some carrying valises full of important documents
        concerning the distribution of souls,
some with their hands folded under their black capes,
        making invocations with their fingers to conjure
        new souls into being;
black flapping drapes of the priests of Paris as
        they go past on their urgent errands.
Beneath their charcoal robes they guard the secret
        purposes of the city, they guard the delicate
        pollen of happiness,
that Paris may flourish and wave gently its leaves in
        the slow air, that its white roots of flesh may
        be moist,
under the dark earth of the priestly garments they
        conserve the deep juices, withholding them, intently
        feeding them,
on their errands, as they go past, and no one talks
        to them, no one looks at them,
as if to pretend that they were not necessary, as if
        to pretend that Paris could flourish without them,
        as if to pretend that their purpose was towards
        some far-off non-Parisian heaven.

At the Mineshaft of a Ghost Town in Southern California

They came with great labour
across a great distance

They dug with great labour
a great distance down.

They took all they could
and went away

leaving as their monument
a great hole.

George Fox, from his Journals

Who had openings within
as he walked in the fields

(and saw a great crack through the earth)

> who went by eye across hedge and ditch toward the spires
> of the steeple-houses, until he came to Litchfield, and
> then barefoot in the market place, unable to contain,
> crying out,

and among friends
of much tenderness of conscience,
of a spirit by which all things might be judged
by waiting
for openings within which would answer each other

(and after that crack, a great smoke)

and in a lousy stinking place, low in the ground,
without even a bed, among thirty convicts, where he
was kept almost half a year, the excrement over the
top of his shoes,

as he gathered his mind inward,
a living hope arose

(and after that smoke, a great shaking)

but when he heard the bell toll to call people to the
steeple-house, it struck at his life; for it was like
a market-bell, to call them that the priest might
sell his wares,
                    such as fed upon words and fed one
another with words until they had spoken themselves
dry, and who raged when they were told, 'The man in
leather breeches is here . . .'

a tender man
with some experience
of what had been opened to him.

'Thighs gripping'

Thighs gripping, hips
moving in pace – her face
suffused – each breath
short and quick
through spread lips,
she is possessed
and lost in the act

alas, trotting
her horse down the lane.

Patrick Waites

The Blue Dog
(*for Gideon*)

It used to work like this:
Teaching school I'd put
My feet up on the master's desk
Stare threatfully across the Daily Mirror
And say to them Today
I want a brown horse
In a green field. That way
They never bothered me.

But now I teach a boy
Who's always running out of paper
Wants fresh water finds fault with
His brush, paints a tractor driven
By his dad (puts trees/flowers/grass/the sky/the sun
Wrestles with demons in the hedgerows
Scatters flocks of birds
Runs screaming from the shadow in the righthand corner
                                    near his house
Whimpers and wipes his nose along his shirt
Cries Sir – cant manage it – the papers turning
Black.

I scold him – not unjustly – and
Help him with the horse
And show him green.

Today he comes to me and
Edges out his painting limp as rag.
The horse, I say, its blue –
The grass all black.
No Sir, he says, thats my dog,
I've got a blue dog.

'The poet's wife'

The poet's wife
    sitting alone at evening
her needle flashing in the pale
        moonlit casement
      gathering up her thoughts in folds of night
the tapestry she sends him
    sparkling brightly on his writing table
      where his tears lie ruined
    among his trophies
       – useless now to gather up the cloth
         & breathe her fragrance:
    she could not come now if he summoned her.
Tiring of embroidery
    she fetched out a pair of her grandmother's
          dancing shoes
       from under the bed
     whispered a few wellworn charms into them
and painted them silver.

Watch her,
      how she runs
     reels through
   the avenues of night
gathering up the folds of darkness
flashing,   flashing

Nicholas Snowden Willey

Les Espaces Interieurs

In the still Autumn and all alone
In the invisible rain, there watching
A small bird who attends the morning light
At the edge of a friendly pond
And at the tangled edge there come to him
Certain circles passing on the water
And the architecture of the morning
Reminds him of what? Circles on a pond
That echo an event somewhere beyond.

All days are certain on a certain day
And in a park of Autumn of a day
Watching a bird at the edge is a way
Somewhere,
And then in that park of Autumn
Silently came a golden spaceship down.

By the fishes unseen, by the bird ignored,
The spaceman for whom nothing remained unexplored
In the green alighting from blue beyond,
And only the ciphers on the surface of the pond
Spoke of a country ever unexplored.

It must be that there are momentous things
Beyond the momentary ends of men,
Somewhere some sizeless circle never changed
By the measuring of our greedy squint.
It must be that there is some quality

That shall survive our scrutinous regard.
Can you bear the speed that will not bear you?
Can you spare the time that will not spare you?

He told me the order that makes the stars to spin
But I forgot to remember clearly for the cold was drawing in.
As far as I remember it was this;
It seemed he had been everywhere
And there was simply no end to it
But he assured me there was a country
Infinitely near which was an endless end
And somewhere while he spoke a bird was encircling
There.

His face was a map of the places of tomorrow
But his eyes showed the currents in uncharted pools of sorrow
And in the wonderful language of obedience he said:
'Whenever from above we survey our lonely zone
Even the horizons of forever are our own.
Even those dear horizons. That is why
I shall no more build cabins in the sky';
But somehow then and there I was aware
The sensible beauty of the Autumn
Was why.

On a certain day all days become certain,
Distance still bright beyond the final curtain.

The world was still. The grass again was green,
Perhaps more clear, at least more clearly seen,
Where me and that singular spaceman had been,
Here in this quiet field I recognize
The amazing country of solitude.

'Pregnant with images'

Pregnant with images, going home,
The dark sky hurrying me on my way,
I remember a cold November day
And a woman pregnant with children,
Or were they images? And I remember
Another day, this time too distinct,
Transparent sunlight and the leaves were red
Of a passion not the children's own
And the children, who are images of what?
And I remember a cold November day.
A little man waiting in the cold,
Certain when nobody looks his way
He does a little dance which is his way
Of keeping the cold away;
But the sun is dancing on the green,
And the day is great with children.

'I have considered considerably'

I have considered considerably.
There's not much object in that sentence.
But then I've considered that going home
Is easier than falling off a log
Midstream. Homing one night I met the dog.
Don't think I'm one who lightly accords
Definite articles to dogs. I'm one
Whose definite article is the sun
All day and all night Anne. If the dog
Spoke English it was gruffly disguised
But as we stood together I surmised

Some furry eloquence in the way he stood
As if he knew the sky bode him no good.
I suppose he was homing too. His advice
Was far from homely. It was like ice
Reminding me that reflection won't suffice
When reflection's moving world ceases to move.
Remember a day. The weather was fine,
Or it was foreboding. In the sunshine,
Or the rain, there crystallized a grand design
That was yours alone and only mine
And we both belonged in the one design.
On that day a sense of belonging
Held sway. There remains only longing
For whatever persuaded grief to resign
To the horizon. When you're ninety-nine
With seconds left you'll see the grand design
And going down will see the trees don't resign
But rage against the sky and beg for a sign.

William Wyatt

Four Haiku

New Years Evening –
in wet socks treading through snow,
cars quickly pass me.

*

Sleeping in the hay,
waking up to the sound of rain –
the angry farmer!

*

A dewy sunrise . . .
the birds singing and dancing
on telegraph poles

*

The water flowing . . .
a white butterfly passes
not hearing a sound.

Four Tanka

Summer

When I awoke this morning
To the sound of wild geese
Squawking in the garden,
I found that the sun was
still shining through my window.

Autumn

The autumn winds blow.
Shepherds sleep and dream
Of dragons and enchanting witches.
While sheep and cattle
Graze completely unaware.

Winter

The old man meditates
On the snow covered mountain.
Wild geese fly south
To catch the sun.

Spring

Who'll come and sit with me
On this fine day?
Only cattle and dung beetles
Seem interested in my company.

On Getting Drunk With Two Swans

drinking a bottle of wine
by the side of the lake,
quietly getting drunk.
grasshoppers and flies
keep me company.
reading poems and gulping wine –
suddenly two swans appear.
happy, i dip some bread into the wine
and offer it to them.

soon my new friends are drunk.
they begin to swim and dance
giddily around the lake,
ducking heads under water.
the three of us madly drunk,
start singing a chorus
to the rising moon.

monk theme

outside the sky
    is macabre

and my thoughts
    dwell on monk
        themes

as he softly plays
    the piano

(& my typewriter
becomes a keyboard)

paintings on
    the walls look
        down & smile

at the progress
    he makes

skipping from note to note
    he tumbles
        like a waterfall

over sad &
    gentle rocks

Michael X

One Flower

While men watched the cities disintegrating
Princesses saw me building our community of new people
who once were write-offs in the old world.
We toiled with a vigour that made them ask,
'for what?' and 'where are you going?' – even 'why?'
It was late in the year and their peace feelers were out –
but we could not hear, our hands were full. The only sounds
were the hammers and saws of the carpenters.
Music we call it. Bombs fell around us.

Those they could gather were thrown in their jails.
We went on. They could not tear down our town.
Their bombs kept raining but one building stood,
it shone like a light amid the ruins.
They could not understand, our foundation was solid.
It is made of the new material – I D E A.

Afterwords

I

1957 – the second hundredth coming of Blake on earth turned
my displaced and under-graduating scholar gipsy's head – to
listen – taste – & witness
    – first fruits of the subsequent decade's farther fields & sub-
terranean zones – now borne aloft to Penguins shore.

Many aspects of the flock I may be supposed to be shepherding
will hardly be touched on in this commentary. I up-end it to
urge the reader – read afresh, take each poet into his breast – a lamb
of Blake. However some may seem unwean'd kids, they share
to my mind a new watchfulness as 'God*s spies' (* 'or whatever
means the good'); self-dedicated, distracted from the 007/TV
way of life, isolated if need be from parents, country, religion –
in the fiery wake of James Joyce – 'forgeing in the smithy of his
soul the uncreated conscience of his race'(which meant a
ruthless renovation of the syllabus his Irish Catholic heritage
had supplied).
At Oxford I saw budding talents buried alive, most elegantly –
taught – to lie; still most persuasively cast in Eliot's calligraphy
of dry bones. 'Between the motion/ And the act . . . Between
the emotion/ And the response' to his poetry, fell the baleful
Shadow – of his influence. Legions of professional hollow men
– brandishing standards of 'The New Criticism' and 'New
Lines' – relaid their trenches, held the muddied field and
apportioned the spoils.
    Their conformist programme, which defined poems as 'the
words on the page', proved a two-dimensional concept-cage:
a counter too rigid and too myopic for those 'to whom the

miseries of the world / are misery, and will not let them rest' –
who seek at the height, with the Shade of Hyperion, to 'think
of the earth'.

Happily (almost imperceptibly, as far as official recognition is
concerned) poetic controls have shifted over these years – to the
unlocked word-hoards of poets who *practise* their art. No place
for them in the educational system – as it stood then, anyway.
In 1958 the *Universities Quarterly* asked Michael Hamburger to
contribute to a symposium on 'The Poet in the University' –
only to withhold his article which posited, from experience,
there's no such animal:

. . . Intrinsically and essentially, the writing of poetry and the teaching
of literature are polar opposites – the one a synthetic process, the
other, nowadays at any rate, very largely an analytical one. If the
tension becomes dialectical, it can be a good thing; but its most
common effect is to turn verse itself into a by-product of literary
criticism, full of literary allusions and – what is much worse – of a
piddling wit, a trivial ingenuity that cries out for the applause of
learned colleagues –

That was 'The Movement'
– that *was*!

Most of us learned, and teach, through less easily formalized
agency
– heard the true voice of feeling from Kenneth Patchen's
Journal of Albion Moonlight and *Sleepers Awake* and poem-
recordings –
& beheld the unfetter'd insurrection of Ginsberg and
Corso through unblinkered eyes – wild flowers growing
straight up – to shame the same different pressed leaves and old
mown grassblades : a green & pleasant land again, suddenly,
in sight of these young men of the new age who put poetry
before all else.

The Introduction to David Wright's anthology of *The Mic
Century: English Poetry 1940–60* (Penguin, 1965), declared tha

. . . American and English poetry is no longer homogeneous, thougl
written in approximately the same language. Contemporary Ameri-
can poetry – which, thanks to the excessive interest taken in it by
American universities, is now an industry rather than an art – seem
to be wandering off in the direction of the decorative, where style and
technique is all . . . It is not that the artist must not be craftsman, bu
that craftsmanship is not all.

Mr Wright is wrong, in that – although his piece is signed
March 1962 – he most obviously had not unwrapped Donald
Allen's parcel of *The New American Poetry 1945–1960* (Grove,
New York, 1960)*
    – nor yet sensed the flexing of other (transatlantic) muscles
'at home'.
        For – if not precisely homogeneous, the experimentalists
on both sides have thrown out (and as frequently been thrown
out by) exactly the demands of immured Academe, for tech-
niques that have outmoded their usefulness, in favour of more
open traditions
    – as of China and Japan – holding the poem vertically as well
as horizontally – to reveal images in light and depth as well as
line;
    – of ceasing to write as soon as the utterance ceases to be a
confession;
    – of the Lyrical Ballads rejection of diction and rhythms
inorganic to what is being said;
    and 'modern jazz' phrasing – as developed, for instance, by
Robert Creeley from Charles Olson's 'Projective Verse'
(*Poetry New York 3*, 1950).

* – condensed & brought up to date with *The New Writing in the USA*
(Penguin, 1967)

But no abstract serendipity informed this selection apart from giving myself, as fully as possible, to the material I unearthed – with Pound's enduring touchstone: 'The best criticism of any work of art comes from the creative writer or artist who does the next job.'

Thus Roy Fisher, in *City*, attempts and achieves something corresponding to the *Paterson* of William Carlos Williams. My concern is more with the differences: Fisher's very particular sense of the British geography, the immediate setting of the poem (his native Birmingham) and his painterly projection thereof. This was traced and extended by Gael Turnbull (in *Kulchur* 7, 1962):

... If Wordsworth and Constable helped to establish a certain 'landscape' in the last century, a work such as CITY is an effort to establish another landscape. ... If Fisher frequently comes to the same material as Williams, it is never from the same starting point or with the same intention. Williams in America is very eagerly concerned to find a 'myth', a 'vision', a 'means' etc., which will give relevance to his city, which will provide him and his poetry with some sort of 'form' through which and by which the man and the city and the poetry can have a community . . For all the focus upon 'Paterson', the city itself as a physical presence continually recedes from the reader. The attention is not so much upon what is actually there as it is upon how it may be useful to the commitment of the poem.

Fisher in the Midlands starts with no such overall concept. Rather he is concerned to perceive and to declare his perception; and that perception must find its own resting place. He looks out into his back garden.

'It is a December afternoon, and it is raining. Not far from the window is a black marble statue of a long-haired, long-bearded old man. . . It is clearly not in its proper place; resting as it does across the moss of the raised border, it is appreciably tilted forward and to one side, almost as if it had been abandoned as too heavy by those who were trying to move it – either in or out.'

... in the happening of an action, all that can be willed is to give oneself as fully as possible to what is going on, to try above all to be true to the closest instinct of the moment, at each moment. Even when its pattern or its meaning may appear utterly lost. Then, later, from another vantage point, we may see what has happened. . . The very language we use is not 'mine' but is only 'ours'; and what we would say, of any material, is shaped by those others both past and present; as it is also shaped by the meanings which are in the material itself, meanings which perhaps we discover rather than create.

Turnbull and Fisher have moved on from Williams, much as several of the Black Mountain poets have – farther still from any prescription of 'craft' beyond the process, the direct dictates of the writing in hand.

2

I'd been approved by tutors to eke out a B.Litt. thesis on my master, whose longer works were at last being more widely read with some understanding. But I shelved it in 1959 and got under way with my own renaissance. The dreaming spires were too much clouded in vapours, their inmates cushioned to sleeping late through incandescence – eternal sunrise of the Heavenly Host – in the comforts of money. Why translate him into their terms, I thought

– & leapt a Glad Day – to kick the entire mental block I'd felt my body and spirit prisoned in. Immersed in poesy and painting I let in clearer glimpses of Blake's vision, of a community of love – in which the fragmented perceptions of individual art-works are but instruments of the vision. Early one morning from my Hinksey cottage retreat I looked to the light as he did – 'not with but through the eyes', windows of the soul – to the bliss of Isaiah's 'Innumerable company' of angels – the 'souls of poets dead and gone' – and yet to be – winging the silver-misted towers, across the vaulted space of centuries

& saw ꞉ the mutual response between people determined to free their spirit can simultaneously give birth to the architecture of that liberation

– as happened that year for the groups who joined to found a review, *New Departures*, together with designer Anna Lovell, composer Cornelius Cardew, playwright John McGrath, David Sladen and yours truly – a-tingling with anticipation of wonder. The title related to Alan Brownjohn's excellent *Departures* – but away from the received ideas it embodied.

The Times Literary Supplement dubbed us 'the most substantial *avant-garde* magazine in Great Britain' – but this concept, also, turned out too bespoke to clothe all our ventures. Understood as an open skull telepathy waveband of innovation and discovery – well and good. But who can insist – amid the imposing plethora of researches too far-flung to be endorsed as a concerted progression, of desperations which challenge all certainty of where one is standing – that a work of art is in front or behind? It starts as a seed, opening to light, and the best it can do is refresh our senses & wake us up to the very life we're living – the life of all creation.

If 'literature is analysis after the event' (Doris Lessing) – *New Departures* was a preview of life: production of the first issue only crystallized our commitment to the contents – only half-alive on the pages.　　　　　Its travelling circus incarnation – '*Live* New Departures' – soon came naturally to transform gilt-edged scenery. In eight years we've mounted some 1,500 shows – involving spoken poetry with jazz, plays, mime, new music, electronics, speeches, film, light/sound projections, sculpture, dance – and with all manner of people and places, many of them hitherto barren of arts.

Ideally there would be no admission charge. The work freely given – out of doors whenever possible – a Blakeheaded *commedia dell' arte* – eliminating the fashionably vaunted gap between art and life, revelling in the extra-mural winds of change. And this organic form 'as proceeding' exquisitely fulfilled our purpose – by means of continuous activation, to construct a *Gesamtweltbild* for all art media to inhabit –

to nourish – perpetual – rebirth – of wonder.

Of the older generation we published & read aloud men with a distinctive *sound*: Schwitters, Burroughs,* Dizzy Gillespie: to discover phrases, words – even letters, have a life of their own – to be looked at and listened to.

McGrath recreated dramatic texts by himself, Beckett and Ionesco – calling them

. . . poems insofar as they express a single lyrical impulse and com-
municate a single lyrical experience in the order of a poem, but plays
insofar as they communicate through two or three or even four
human voices and through the action of human bodies. On the page
these poems are so many unlaid eggs: demanding voice; demanding
meaning; demanding movement. On the page they are symbols of an
experience, pointers towards action, concepts of form. In this
programme they will be given identity and reality, the incon-
trovertible precision of events. Too many poems are old and unevent-
ful. Not events. These are.

Cardew encouraged ensembles – which increasingly included non-musicians – to 'read' the indeterminate scores prepared by himself, Boulez, Stockhausen, Cage, Feldman, Wolff and Young, as points of departure for improvisation:

* We were I believe the first to publish Burroughs in Britain – and
inadvertently did his first cut-ups for him! Others featured in *New
Departures* magazine were Paul Ableman, Patrick Bowles, Corso,
Creeley, Donald Davie, Om de Haulleville, John Fuller, Ginsberg,
Hamburger, Heliczer, Hans Helms, Hollo, Langston Hughes, Kerouac,
Kops, Mitchell, O'Connor, Queneau, Herbert Read, Graham Reynolds,
Silkin, Sillitoe, Stevie Smith, August Stramm, Stefan Themerson,
Yevtushenko and Mary Lou Williams; the painters Franciszka Themer-
son, Burri, Davie, Pasmore, Picasso and Rauschenberg; & the composers
George Brecht, John Cage and La Monte Young.

Anything written down must be brought to life, and it can be brought to life in an infinite variety of ways, and it can be brought to an infinite variety of lives, even . . .

It didn't matter that we were unsettled in any one place, finding – as Henry Miller had – 'What is not in the open street is false, derived, that is to say, *literature*': which is superfluous when it's only *about* something: at 'Live New Departures' it became something in its own right, and therefore essential.

A visiting Martian would never guess from the bulk of twentieth-century writing that men were made to talk to one another. Patchen reckoned that many 'Novelists talk about their characters. . . because they have nothing to say about themselves.' The stylized accomplishments which make 'selling lines' 'readable' leave them correspondingly un-readoubtable. I don't mean the real artists, composers, wordsmiths who aspire to the condition of Joyce, whose 'Anna Livia' record we played repeatedly. & ourselves likewise recoined words, freed original meanings – to be understood again – *hierarchitectitiptitoplofically* – !

An absolute of vigour, honesty and responsibility became the only law in the fluctuating context of our sessions – at which about two-thirds of the poets in this book first subjected their work to the public test, often hard by the American pioneers. Programmes of 'poetry that jumps the book', I sometimes called them – for squareness is a shape in which no human audience occurs! & books – however beautiful – are more and more distant branches, and not the roots of culture communication.

We went on the road in spontaneous accord, to revive the oral traditions by which the word had resounded through the ages – long before the Gutenberg Galaxy began spinning its webs of obliquity: Beauty's speech was restored to the poet's mouth!
Pete Brown and I met in a field at the Beaulieu Jazz Festival

of 1960 & immediately hitched to Edinburgh, scatting out 'chase-chorus' improvisations en route; to unleash the resultant dialogues in the city's parks, squares and cafes alongside Heliczer, Hollo, Kops, Dave Ball, Alan Jackson – kindred spirits – we took off & got going with there and then.

Jackson picks up the story of these 'beyond the fringe' jam sessions, which were to be a colourful highspot of the Edinburgh scene for several summers following:

. . . they came up and had the readings in 'The Cellars' under the bus station . . . and I began reading out of my book. Well, the cellars were fantastic – all sorts of people – drunk sailors falling down the stairs, and you had to command the audience – you had to make them listen as well as just read. After about four days of this I began to get the feel of what words could do with people there, and I began writing things, more conversational things and by the end of that festival I was not reading out of the book at all. I was reading things I'd written during the festival which belonged to that kind of atmosphere.

It is amazing – the variety of people who are reading now – the different things they can do with words . . . somehow the things come together – the ease and the tone that you get for reading become united with a kind of deep contact. When, say, Mitchell is reading, you realise that the poem on the page is just a . . . it's like a score for music, because when Adrian reads it, it's quite different: it's got rhythm, a song intonation, the blues theme. You never know it's on the page unless you're a very sort of wise chap.

When your turn comes you're glad to read – there's such a pleasant mood been created . . . people are glowing – I mean, it's like blowing in jazz, you know. You want to get up and blow –

The next year a *TLS* leader had noticed

. . . There is a nucleus of poets who are starting to treat the writing and the delivery of a poem as two stages in a single process – Mr Adrian Mitchell is the outstanding example – and this in turn leads to a new view of the popular media . . The actual presence of an audience, provided it is alert and responsive, forces the poet-reader to take greater care about the meaning of his words, while a reasonably strong formal pattern is almost essential in any poem that is going to be read aloud . .　There is also a growing realisation that poetry can be entertaining. Poets like Mr Logue, Mr Horovitz and others have done something most valuable in luring jazz-conscious audiences to listen to genuine poetry and find that they can get the same kind of fun, and even the same kind of kick out of it, as they get from music. The next decade could see a real break-through here.

All kinds of artists have been uniting their resources – & each feels personally answerable, to help invent a future for the arts (and hence for society) without reference to the backwash of nineteenth-century materialism which continues to sustain catastrophic struggles for power.

Lively magazines proliferated – most of them still sprouting in Charing Cross Road, The Turret Bookshop and Indica – reinforced with readings and manifestations all over the country. The Wild Hawthorn Press bloomed in Edinburgh, whilst Lee Harwood travelled through *Night Scene*, *Night Train*, *Soho*, *Horde*, *Darazt* & *Tzarad*. *Poetmeat* sprang up – with *Screeches for Sounding* – in Blackburn, *Dust* was raised in Leeds, a *Phoenix* in Liverpool, *Outburst* in Hackney, *New Voice* in Kent; *Migrant* from Worcester – *Move* from Preston – *Eleventh Finger* from Brighton – *Origins/Diversions* from Carshalton – *Whisper* & *shout* from Derby . . . *The Resuscitator* in Wessex! *Insomnia* in Peterborough – *Priapus* in Berkhamsted . . . Eventually even a *Soltice* in Cambridge, *New Measure* at Oxford, *Guerilla* in Clapham and *Albion* in West 11. *The Dis-inherited* of Cheltenham recently dropped the 'Dis'; & the ambitious Ferry, Fulcrum, Goliard and Trigram presses are permeating the atmosphere with brave new volumes each season.

Towns with a thriving underworld of clubs and musicians and art students, multiracial late night populations and voluntary unemployment, tend to breed more intelligent, fresh and sensitive audiences for this 'new view of the popular media' than college or literary platforms – which are frequently prejudiced, blasé, jaded. Dialect and regional speech are revivified, & the once obligatory superior accents of BBC and bossman forgotten (except when they're the poet's genuine inside accent) at the regular readings that have been presented at the ICA and Ben Uri Galleries, neighbourhood crypts & arts workshops, in London libraries, pubs and theatres by *Tribune*, *Ambit*, *Writer's Forum*, the Dulwich *Outposts* & other journals; by Better Books, Brighton's Unicorn and Nottingham's Trent Bookshop; and round restaurants, halls, dives & barns of greater London & UFO provincial zones by poets, rebels, anarchists, clowns, in and out of jobs or scholar's gowns.

One such is Tom Pickard of Newcastle who 'were on the doale for three year' – at 18, in 1964, and decided to consecrate the Morden Tower Book Room: This is a tower on the old city wall which had fallen to disuse except as a rehearsal room and meeting place for Guilds. The designation 'Book Room' enabled Pickard to hire the tower from the Council for only 10s. a week. The Tynesiders responsive to the experimental writing in which he specializes were too young and broke to cover the costs of keeping even this up, so he sought aid from the North East Arts Association and got it. Basil Bunting – Northumbria's long neglected epic poet – and Richard Hamilton the painter collaborated with Pickard, floating out a loose leaf review, *King Idas Watch Chain* – which has now come to life in the form of a rocking words-&-music troupe. (The enterprising NEAA have also rescued Jon Silkin and *Stand* after ten years of martyrdom. More's the pity this has not set a precedent, as yet, for chancellors elsewhere to open up their vaults.)

Came '65, and Ginsberg saw in Liverpool –

Albion, Albion, your children dance again
Jerusalem's rock established in the basements of Satanic Mills . . .

Several of the younger poets are clearer spokesmen than the groups (& stay ahead – beyond numbers) for the mixed multitudes who are presently animating, intermingling and loosening the perimeter divisions between poetry – jazz – blues – raga & modern classical music in the new solar sound-systems of beat caverns, pop charts, and psychedelic 'trips'. Their poems, with the more wordwhile hits, are truly popular songs – ones which reflect (so be they banned on the radio) the way people are actually living; which dig at the realities behind the screen, the enforced dreams of our society – or elicit more meaningful ones.

I've never come to miss the sophistications that are cast off in sparking direct contact with a different houseful, circuit of listeners every week. It's a public that generally pays scant attention to the written word, being prepossessed – not with the past, or the future – but with N O W

– meaning they'll watch and give ear, intently. & when turned on and tuned in to real poetry, they can never quite drop out.

A poet – if poet he be – must also & at once be truth-teller. Sometimes the most sincere jazzmen, folk and pop-singers get tied to the *Business* of entertainment: – just another of the scenes we're out to change, setting our foreheads against all the public duplicities by which we're expected to abide.

So far from translating these brands of audience expectation, the object of 'Live New Departures' was always that taste be refined, responses sharpened. So the tide of swelling doubt as to the use of poetry which has bogged down so many promising writers – & drowned a few – since the Renaissance collapse of the medieval synthesis, is turned back at reading after reading, – each one partly extemporized and uniquely *there* as Miller's open street. The aural, visual and situational elements combine with the unpredictable interaction between the manifold

performers and auditors to throw up a theatre on the spot –
transcending the old form of theatre because what is happening
is really happening!

As if by contrast, the most publicized sector of the 'break-
through' – the Merseyside Blow Up – has been marketed via
the guillotine channels of the pop industry – at the expense of
what really happened. Brian Patten* is the man most res-
ponsible for building the *actual* Liverpool Scene with his
plangent erotic saxophonetrance voice, & a scrutable sincerity
– evoked also in his littlest, purest of little mags – *Underdog* –
which is not even mentioned in the glossy hard-bound slab
of bookmaking that exploits the blurb. Nor is the Crane
Theatre concert of 1960 – the first large-scale informal poetry
show in the North – given by Brown, Hawkins and myself
with the jazz partnership of Dick Heckstall-Smith and Art Reid's
band. Thus might bite, bark and hair of the dog be blunted,
struck dumb, cut off – made palatable as a chi chi above-
board investment. . . but for the true voice's surviving truth.
Adrian Henri and Roger McGough are now become out-
spokenly pop artistes – & very good ones: but the hard core
of working 'public' poets worthy the name still have less in
common with either pop painters or pop musicians than they
do with the unbroken Young Christian Monk Getz Dizzy line
of rhythm & blues & roots & bop –

3

Jazz: sacred river, deeply embedded in the american idiom, was
a seminal influence for many of us: underground movement,
living mythology and international language of our upbring-
ing: which addressed its primal messages to the whole world –

* The work of Patten, Jackson and others would naturally have been in-
cluded in this book, were it not already well represented in the Penguin
Modern Poets series & elsewhere.

& through which all could speak. The opening frontiers that evolved when negro delta essence welled has fused (with astonishingly little confusion) word and music writers, performers, listeners & readers into instantaneous connexion – however widely dispersed in ethnic, musical and literary traditions.

Its first experimental phase – the bebop of the '40s & '50s, which applied all the vitality of folk art with subtleties as complex as the 'highest' European music – remains the correlative for divers aesthetic communities that preceded it. Charlie Parker said

Music is your own experience, your own thoughts, your wisdom. If you don't live it, it won't come out of your horn. They teach you there's a boundary line to music. But, man, there's no boundary line to art . . .

The boppers' recognition that the artistically impoverished conditions which moulded Traditional and standard styles had been rendered obsolete is echoed by the release of poetry from the dusty iambic grooves of book (society) culture. Witness (Sobriety) Kerouac

– If possible write 'without consciousness' in semi-trance (as Yeats' later 'trance writing') allowing subconscious to admit in own uninhibited interesting necessary and so 'modern' language what conscious art would censor, and write excitedly, swiftly, with writing-or-typing-cramps, in accordance (as from centre to periphery) with laws of orgasm, Reich's 'beclouding of consciousness'. *Come* from within, out – to relaxed and said.

('Essentials of Spontaneous Prose' – *Evergreen Review* 5, New York)

– & Corso's sense of the analogy:

. . . When Bird Parker or Miles Davis blow a standard piece of music, they break off into other own-self little unstandard sounds – well, that's my way with poetry – X, Y and Z, call it automatic – I call it a standard flow (because at the offset the words are standard) that is intentionally distracted diversed into my own sound. Of course many will say a poem on that order is unpolished, etc – that's just what I want them to be – because I have made them truly my own – which is inevitably something NEW – like all good spontaneous jazz, newness is acceptable and expected – by hip people who listen.

(Preface to 'Gasoline' – *City Lights*, San Francisco, 1957)

Just as the jazz horn is an extension of the man breathing through it, so is the pen   the flow of words   the tongue itself. Just as jazz is not a Music but a way of playing, so is this new oral poetry another way of speaking, delivering one's own brief in time in one's own indestructibly personal way – tho it speak faster than intellection, forgetful of self.

One of the greatest forces in jazz, from its hybrid origins in New Orleans and before, has been its capacity for uninhibited intercourse with other forms of expression.

There's a strong line of dissent from the poetry of the workshouts, gospel-hymns and blues singers, through that of Louis Armstrong, Vachel Lindsay, Auden &c, to Charles Mingus, Patchen or LeRoi Jones. But a lot of jazz 'proper' was turned in on itself of late. – The specially composed poetry placed in apposition & in conjunction with it at 'Live New Departures' and allied whirligigs let fresh airs into the suffocated record-garages – let the wild lip-to-touch stir up soft-warbling winds, new sounds that blew space open: poem-seedlings flew, alighted – & grew – bright gold aloft old pruned branches. New combinations descanted out, unpenn'd – *new* jazz, wingsped afloat the highways again – and again and again and again. – To open new vistas, that kept us all sane!

Rexroth and Ferlinghetti married their poetry to jazz in San Francisco in order

. . . to get poetry out of the hands of the professors and the squares. If we can get poetry out into the life of the country, it can be creative.

And their bandleader, Bruce Lippincott, sensibly

. . . set up as the first rule – listen to each other. And second – respond with our instruments as emotionally as possible to the *words* of the poem and also the pre-arranged form. Such as . . . for this many lines we will have the drums swelling and rolling and the bass will enter at the bottom and play bowed. Pre-arranged that way – letting the instruments know when they are to enter and what they are to do. If we listen to each other, we can get a kind of question-and-answer thing going on underneath, all without any key. It comes down to a new and different approach to jazz. The idea of responding, not in a pre-ordained way, but in a question-and-answer sort of a relative-pitch way. . . You give it a new dimension with a much stronger visual element, rather than just an auditory one. Any really aware musician is attracted by this.

(*Jam Session*, ed. Ralph Gleason, Peter Davis, 1958)

Several Americans utilized the partnership as a fad in the late '50s, but remained men of letters in their practice compared to those of us who put our trust in 'proper sowing', and only published through underground presses. Jerry Hooker wrote of the first (& only?) exchange-poem for jazz – 'Blues for the Hitchhiking Dead', by Brown and me, at its first public declamation with the New Departures Quintet* –

The word danced off the page, where it has lain crucified for too long, and blended with the music in such a way that the result was neither poetry nor jazz, but jazzpoetry.

. . . A resurrection that seemed to chime in tune with the nascent audio-visual culture. And gradually to remind literati about the versions of Beowulf as laid down for exams being as remote from its dissemination in the dark ages as the printed text of a traditional blues is from its first evolution – as sung – in

* – a group of Britain's most adventurous modernists – Stan Tracey, Jeff Clyne, Laurie Morgan, Les Condon and Boddy Wellins – in their (then) preferred formation.

the deep South . . .   & awake again to Homer, & the undying anonymous body of early English lyrics and ballads. Now that the poet's voice looks to be recovering the crucial means of handing on poetic tradition, records as well as books provide a means of assessing and preserving this development. But even these may in years to come serve only as relics of a thoroughly reformed social art; they can't contain the real-life life of the poems which – given free rein – might subtly evaporate the dominion of commercial interests, aggressive nationalisms and governments as we know them.

According to Francis Newton,

Cynics have claimed that 'poetry-and-jazz' is a mere gimmick to increase the audience for poetry by drawing on the larger one for jazz, but they are wrong. There is an affinity between all the avant-gardes anyway, and a special one between jazz and the non-rational neo-romanticism which defines the task of writing as 'one man trying to tell another man of the events in his own heart', and certainly between Whitmanesque rhetoric and the less disciplined jazz solo. It is true (to quote the special issue of 'New Departures' on this subject) that jazz rests on speech rhythms, and that 'in the best contemporary solo there seems to be a lacuna where the words should be. . .   The soloist is playing a mute poem in the free rhythms that language assumes. Consciously or unconsciously, he is taking on the burden of missing words. . . . Billie Holiday says she grew out of Lester Young's saxophone playing . . . without his wordless poems built on the basic impulses in the songs, the lyrics would have frozen her. A verbal equivalent to the up-to-the-minute awareness expressed by new wave music is supplied in up-dated ballads & blues, blasts, routines, incantations, hymns & anti-ads . . .' Thanks to the present crisis in modern jazz, at least one important outwork has now been stormed

– this, in reference to the residencies of our Jazz Poetry Septet at Ronnie Scott's Club and the Marquee. The crisis coincided substantially with that in 'modern' poetry, in that its practitioners were no longer singing, nor even metaphorically talking to one another; but ringing exhaustive permutations of technical niceties, 'writing' – however brilliantly – to themselves – out of touch with the basic 'hear me talkin' to ya' cry & YES of jazz. Vocals have virtually atrophied, and soloists unremittingly hide behind their horns like the university wits behind their research – to the demise of both: unless their roots are nourished – the interplay of voice and instrument at community celebrations.

What, in fine, is realized in the live transposition of jazz-poems (e.g. 'Dreaming the Hours Away', 'Man-to-Man Blues', 'Hunga', Patten 'Dreaming of a White Smethwick') is dovetailing Apollo's lyre back into the lyric – and the original, telling lyric back into jazz; stretching our techniques to resolve a present-day equation of Leadbelly, Bessie Smith, Woody Guthrie, etc; which would be well & done if singers and lyrists apart from the tribe of Dylan had the heart to do anything, with the *long* breath – the visibly sustained creative stance – Bringing It All Back Home – in words. With virtuoso guitarists such as Davy Graham and John Renbourn, as well as the ND bands – Brown and I, Patten and Pickard pitch jazz-infected words & instrumentally phrased sounds in tempo, rhythm and harmony to their poetically inflected chords & instrumentally phrased sounds – swapping breaks & solo embellishments and sharing choruses whenever we feel in unison –

zonked & measured stories, sound-poems and themes for impromptu variation. We've also joined issue with totally unscripted British, European and American free-form musicians – Dave Tomlin, George Kisch, David Izenzon, Ornette Coleman – to unframe words and notes from all conventional metre, arrangement, mood, or conception of harmony, discipline, language. So that the music means something again and poetry speaks openly, to all.

Directions the 'break-through' is taking were indicated by
Mitchell in '66:

There's a natural hunger for poetry in everyone. But the invention
of printing and glum-headed education managed to cut poems down
to dwarf size. Poetry eating became a solitary, rare and almost per-
verted occupation. In this century people became so jumpy they could
hardly nibble. But one by one and four by four, poets broke out of
their cells. Edith Sitwell tried. Dylan Thomas made it and was pun-
ished to death. Ginsberg and Ferlinghetti and Yevtushenko opened
the gates and out we rushed, blinking and drinking in the light. In the
past five, six, seven years more and more British poets have been
stomping the island giving adrenaline transfusions in cellars, town
halls, schools, clubs, pubs, theatres, anywhere. Whenever enough
people knew that poetry was around they came, grabbed it and
started chewing. So it's no surprise that 6,000 plus came to the Albert
Hall feast. It wasn't the beginning of anything, it was public proof
that something had been accelerating for years. Within another ten
years I hope that plenty of advertising posters (& neon signs) will be
replaced by poems (& neon poems), that poets will chant from the
TV screen and poems leap among the stories in daily papers. I want
poetry to bust down all the walls of its museum/tomb and learn to
survive in the corrosive real world. The walls are thick but a hundred
Joshuahs are on the job.

– Of course it suits many fine poets (Cunliffe, Finlay, Raworth)
to keep their stillness at a distance from the madding throngs.
For many others poetic commitment means social commit-
ment – especially to the youngest, whose diet is – despite their
boasted independence in the U K and U S – over-exposed to the
mercies of hidden persuaders. I don't want verse mass-produced
and fed to queues from conveyor-belts – simply know the
communications media as an unavoidable message-massage of
our mass age; arts we most value should therefore be presented
through them, so far as they can be, without fear they be
diluted. At readings large or small, broadcast or televised, the
medium can usually (endowed with a modicum of skill) be

contracted to the one we're all born with – which poetry is born of – the human voice and body.

Even the jazzpoems are first sketched in solitude, and we've learned the futility of preparing any kind of illusionistic façade for sensation-seeking spectators. At best the seemingly inbuilt partitions of back-reference, admiration and criticism are toppled by the immediate involvement of everyone present. Fellow feeling between poets plants an Eden of new consciousness: in Blakean image, the lion (energy) slays the monster of mental operations & lies down with the lamb (spirit) – to rise again, as one man – 'to smite the land with the rod of his mouth'; or nurture it with wells of song.

Once there were bards, and the bards did something wondrous – they provided literature for the illiterate. The bards evolved into poets, and the poetry which had been their means became their end. It didn't seem to matter very much while 'everyone' was literate anyway. But semi-literacy, which is where people go when they're not illiterate any more, is in some ways a worse blight . . .

(Robert Christgan in Cheetah, Summer 1967)

– Which is where many people are at now: high time for bards again – operating at ground level – that is heaven. Sing Hallelluia the new apocalypse of troubadors – jointing the bonds of Reader & Congregation and the classic Afric jazz pattern of call & response – individual and collective swinging together in harmony. For all that none of us may be 'folk' in 1968, the nuts of oralism is still what Langston Hughes – late lamented father of jazz-poetry – has described as

. . . the common loneliness of the folk-song that binds one heart to all the others – and all the others to the one who sings the song.

The margin between verse and song was widened by Eliot's cerebral intonations & his boosting of the school of Donne for having taught the lyric to think. Orpheus, Caedmon, Petrarch,

Wyatt – the scops & harpists & minstrels have been intel-
lectualized into history by dons and dilettantes; and yet
the heightened strains of everyday talk, dream and behaviour
wedded to poetic diction in American Negro Blues, beat poetry
and folk-rock have begun to convince even them that poets can
think deeply – and yet sing music: then lo

> – those brave translunary things
>   the first poets had!

4

The first International Poetry Incarnation at Albert Hall was
conceived, at a week's notice: to affirm – a purely poetic space.
The three leading communist poets – Andrei Voznesensky,
Pablo Neruda, and Pablo Fernandez the Cuban – who had
been delighted by the prospect, nonetheless withdrew at the
last moment. – Ginsberg had just been deported from Cuba,
and then bounced by the Czechs (after being voted King of the
May Festival by 100,000 students of Prague) –

naturally, for I am of Slavic parentage and a Buddhist Jew
who worships the Sacred Heart of Christ the blue body of Krishna
      the straight back of Ram
The beads of Chango the Nigerian singing Shiva Shiva in a manner
      which I have invented,
and the King of May is a middleeuropean honour, mine in the xx
      century
despite space ships and the Time Machine, because I heard the voice of
      Blake in a vision,
and repeat that voice . . .

– But Neruda was reputedly worried that the King of May
might take off his clothes! Thus spake the business of good
governmental censorship – the 'Earth's Answer' in Blake – to
interpose and nail down yet again the obscene boundaries,
chaining even the tongues of poets to its 'Eternal Bane' – party
lines, protocol non-alignments – 'That free Love with bondage
bound.' Not so the sixteen other poets, *un*bound from eight

countries – who did ignore or smash all the other barriers with space-age confessions & elegies & paeans & exhortations whose feedback goes on circling the globe for suns and moons and stars to come.

A notion of what happened that lovely midsummer night may be derived from the film *Wholly Communion* (& also the booklet of the same title – which contains stills from it, and complete texts of the poems it shows in action – including a passionate 'Extorted Divagation' by Voznesensky – in Hollo's translation – which Ginsberg read directly to the Russian's gripped presence): though – for anyone who was there – this merely exposes the glaring weakness of cinema: an event which was at least three-dimensional is reduced to a (literally) framed photo-reproduction. Most of the poems have been slashed to shreds in the editing, and the delicate relationships, conflicts and love between the poets are pushed out of focus on sale to the sham realities of 'locked out' consumer-consciousness.   What did happen – for whoever suspended disbelief – is that poem after poem resonated mind-expanding ripples of empathy – uncut and precious stones in a translucent pool. The buds of a spreading poetry internationale, the esperanto of the subconscious sown by dada & the surrealists & the beats bore fruit – a renewal of light, of 'the Holy Word / That walk'd among the ancient trees' – made flesh.

Instead of programme notes, ten of us – John Esam, Harry Fainlight, Ferlinghetti, Fernandez, Ginsberg, Paolo Lionni, Daniel Richter, Alex Trocchi, Simon Vinkenoog and I – got our heads together the night before and improvised an Invocation, prefaced by six lines from 'Jerusalem' (for the initial moving spirit of our cooperative was the transmission, through Ginsberg, of the heritage of Blake):

England!   awake! awake! awake!
  Jerusalem thy Sister calls!

        *   *   *   *

And now the time returns again:
    Our souls exult, & London's towers
Receive the Lamb of God to dwell
    In England's green & pleasant bowers.

World declaration hot peace shower! Earth's grass is
free! Cosmic poetry Visitation accidentally happening
carnally! Spontaneous planet-chant Carnival! Mental
Cosmonaut poet-epiphany, immaculate supranational
Poesy insemination!

        Skullbody love-congress Annunciation,
duende concordium, effendi tovarisch illumination,
Now! Sigmatic New Departures Residu of Better
Books & Moving Times in obscenely New Directions!
Soul revolution City Lights Olympian lamb-blast!
Castalia centrum new consciousness hungry
generation Movement roundhouse 42 beat
apocalypse energy-triumph!

        You are not alone!
Miraculous assumption! O Sacred Heart invisible
insurrection! Albion! awake! awake! awake! O
shameless bandwagon! Self-evident for real naked
come the Words! Global synthesis habitual for this
Eternity! Nobody's Crazy Immortals Forever!

Amazingly – and amazed – I felt we lived up to this high-
sounding prologue, with a sacramental jubilee that uncovered
an ideal america – united states of being. Relatively few read
their poems, but everybody heard the call. As Ernst Jandl, the
Austrian sound-poet said, 'No one was one, but we each were
the thousands, re-shaped in one beautiful body of voices and
echoes, with Allen Ginsberg our soul' – arch-celebrant, with
flowing beard mantic hair radiant eyes hand-pointing drunken
bear arms frolicy lolloping legs – suddenly crouched in con-
templation, clashing finger-cymbals to bell in the readings
with a Tibetan mantra – bringing us to surface together, egg-

man, opening our mouths, hearts and minds; navigating our course in the persona of a too-long exiled biblical prophet – though his message was disposed more broadly for the occasion than any frocked priest would allow, even in his final compassionate prayer from 'Be Kind' – a psalm he'd summoned up 48 hours earlier:

Tonite let's all make love in London as if it were 2001 the years of
    thrilling god –
and be kind to the poor soul that cries in a crack of the pavement
    because he has no body –
our prayers to the ghosts and demons, the lackloves of Capitals and
    frightened Congresses, who make sadistic noises on the radio –
Statute destroyers and tank captains, unhappy murderers in Mekong
    and Congo –
That a new kind of man has come to his bliss to end the cold war
    he has borne against his own kind flesh since the days of the snake.

The gathering was acclaimed by some as the greatest stimulus for poetry this century.*

---

*– Robert Gittings was inspirited to record
'Poets at the Royal Albert Hall, June 11th, 1965' – *An Impression*:

It began with the flowers. The solid arena, the mausoleum,
Frowned as the poets came,
With a weight of unpromising architecture, blank waste walls
To smash the wave.
Then they started to give away flowers. The flowers took over, took
    charge,
Permeated the brick,
The steps, the entrance, the foyer, swamped ticket-tearers, pro-
    gramme-sellers;
Something unheard of
Happened. The crushed narcissi, gladioli, iris, scented and trans-
    formed
The whole plush area
To growing life. From bruised juicy stalks they rooted again,
The tiered seats their soil.

Chairbacks and barriers began to sprout. Vine-tendrils appeared and
    clung.
A procession in the aisles
Had panthers in it, leopards not needing a leash, wandering among
The friendly incomers.
Nothing distinct occurred but the occasion had become religious,
With drums and bells
And chants that shut out the bright efficient western day,
The false world.
Here was a world for the poets to exhibit a world of truth,
With thousands sharing,
The world where every word could be spoken, the true poets truthful,
Serious, being heard:
And more poets than those billed on the programme and speaking
Were evident there,
An audience sprinkled with verse-makers, come to applaud and
    encourage
And cheer them home,
Names from the anthologies actually present in flesh and blood,
Their own faces,
Not the mask of biography and piety, but the imperfect,
Human and unique:
Keats with his long protuding upper lip and delighted stare,
Really rejoicing,
Shelley, snapping his fingers and shouting excitedly, standing up
Tall and pale,
And Rocky-face, the revolutionary man from the north, before
He became a sheep's head;
His friend, the grey-eyed somnambulist, measuring his opium
Against modern mescalin,
All were there: a crowd from the Mermaid Tavern had taken off
    doublet
And Tudor dress,
And were acting a play impromptu, their chief mover being he
Who played the King.
So the poets read; and while the trickery and policy of governments
Shuddered to a standstill,
The whole great grounded ship of poetry burst into leaf and grape,
And dolphins curved and leapt.

A *TLS* leader – 'Stirring Times' – said we 'made literary history by a combination of flair, courage and seized opportunities', and an unprecedented host of poetry lovers was refreshed by the overnight transformation of London's notorious bastion of cultural reaction into a Temple of the Muses.

The Hall's Manager, however, was trying to ban the men who read then, and at the succeeding year's New Moon Carnival, from ever appearing there again – trying, indeed, to forbid *any* poetry reading under Albert's dome – because 'four-letter words associated with Lady Chatterley' were spoken: 'I don't want that sort of filth here. Would you send your teenage daughter to hear that sort of thing?'

– What a character-istic drag on the new energy for one of the island's best venues 'in the round' to be restricted, just for the sake of its name, to only those artistic displays which comply with homage to Victorian Puritanism! Poets have always laid bare their basic nature – unto the utmost extremes of love and hate – in the most expressive language they know; and young people relate this to the facts of life as they live it – not a sexually reactionary Georgian novel! It's the insistent refusal of the old and conservative to accept this – if not for themselves, for their sons and daughters – that cements the walls of mutual deception or despair.

To millions of the (overgrown) children of the midcentury, 'Something is Happening and You Don't Know What It Is, Do You, Mr Jones?' Nothing that exists can be hidden – nor needs to be – from the 'new kind of man', original man and muse – 'the only gods, the only lords of Kingdoms of Feeling, Christs of their own living ribs'; given their trigger release through the new kind of writing impelled by '*Howl*'; in which Ginsberg turned his back on what he'd conscientiously primed as notes for possible poems 'to follow my romantic inspiration – Hebraic-Melvillean bardic breath, I thought I wouldn't write a *poem*, but just write what I wanted to without fear, let my imagination go, open secrecy, & scribble magic lines from my real mind – sum up my life'.

– Writing which brands 'bomb' the most obscene word, as it represents the most obscene impulse in our civilization – and all the concomitant obscenities which drone on – apparently usurping the media (but this doesn't mean the *word* should be banned). Public feeling is inevitably aroused by work that speaks out loud and clear against cruel, violent public obscenities very few can really believe in. It's more than a conflict between generations: Neil Oram sees 'What is going on, is a war between those who believe in poetry, and those who don't.'

Kenneth Tynan has been attacked for observing that

... Poverty and starvation, which afflict more than half the human race, enrage us – if at all – only in a distant generalized way; yet we are roused to a state of vengeful fury when Lenny Bruce makes public use of harmless, fruitful syllables like 'come' (in the sense of orgasm) and 'fuck'. Where righteous indignation is concerned, we have clearly got our priorities mixed up ...

– In themselves the swear-words flout only convention, but the overall effect of most of the poetry which employs them liberally, like Bruce's surreal-real fables & improvisations, was/is – revaluation: to shock audiences into perception – of the ubiquitous managerial assault on human dignity and sensibility and words of love – *and that we can withstand it* –

5

For the Lord said unto Ginsberg

The individual soul is under attack and for that reason a 'beat' generation existed and will continue to exist under whatever name

Rosey generation lost or as Kerouac once prophecied Found until it is found. The soul that is. And a social place for the soul to exist manifested in *this* world. By soul I mean that which differs man from thing, i.e. person – not mere mental consciousness – but feeling bodily consciousness. As long as this tender body feeling is under attack there will continue the expression in Art of the scream or weep or supplication the EXPRESSION in one form or other of that infinite Self – which still feels through the smog of Blakeansatanic war mills and noise of electric sighs & spears which is XX century mass communication.

Uniquely the art work is of one single hand, the mark of individual person ... Poetry: the renaissance of individual sensibility carried thru the vehicle of individualized metrics – individuality differentiating not conforming – that's accomplished.

– & so the 'beat', 'afterbeat', 'underground', individualist writers are being read, enjoyed, understood, felt – taken as seriously as they take themselves – and seen to be far removed from the exhibitionist soup-kitchen sages of masscult captions. It is their odes and chronicles that proclaim the explicitly spiritual revolt, the deliverance from his shadow side modern man has craved for fifty years and more.

Musing on Rimbaud's 'Time of the Assassins', Miller found that – mentally – modern man is still on all fours today, 'And what he fears most – God pity him – is his own image ...' We're confronting ourselves, jumping and pushing (our minds) as high as we can – 'without fear', knowing there's nothing to fear; taking up, with Ginsberg and with each other, the eternal themes of Inferno, Purgatory and Paradise, the marriages of heaven & hell, reason & energy, conscious & unconscious – in new systems of our own making; supplemented – in their application – by the voices of all bards 'Who present, Past and Future see'.

The continuous tradition of Israel's tents, understood as art and poetry, survives with the power to lead us and our des-

cendants away from the yoke of Mammon. The poetic trans-
cendence of western rationalism is illustrated by Blake's
'Elijah': the prophet who gives his cloak of inspiration to
Elisha, symbolizing the poet who grasps the everlasting truths
of the imagination – the divine presence in man – reveals it, and
hands it on.

In the light of Jerusalemic mythology, catalysts like Fer-
linghetti, heralds like Corso and a high-priest like Ginsberg
were indeed called for to revive Albion today. England had
need of Miltonics – strong confident voices, to purge the
atmosphere of slick or ambiguous non-sounds. She seemed the
veritable 'fen of stagnant waters' – her obtaining philosophies
sunk in 'irritable reaching after fact and reason' – controlled by
logical and linguistic analysis; her arts in the anxious vicelike
grip of surface naturalism, & poesy tied down by abstract law,
the type of Urizen ('Your reason' + the Greek 'limiting
power') – unregenerate commonsensical enemies of light. Her
literary giants mere Goliaths of advertising, her brightest sparks
in the deathly stupor of materialism. The situation is directly
comparable to that of Blake's *Jerusalem* – well summarized by
H. M. Margoliouth:*

– Albion, personified England or Britain, now stands for Man, the
symbolism of the part for the whole. Man is asleep and dreaming.
Clear vision will only come when he wakes. . . Here, as in *Milton*,
Albion is dead to Eternity. He believes in the evidence of his senses
and the survival of *qui peut*. Jerusalem, which is his soul's instinctive
longing for and knowledge of Eternal Life, is a 'Phantom of the over
heated brain'. This disaster which has overtaken Albion, the Fall, may
in one aspect be likened to the disaster which overtook the fabled
island Atlantis when the ocean overwhelmed it. The Altantic, there-
fore, regularly symbolizes the Sea of Error which separates Europe
from America, on which so many had cast longing eyes in the revolu-
tionary years.

* in *William Blake*, Oxford University Press, 1951.

The apprehension of a vast dread change which would blot out war and exploitation, and free the oppressed millions for brotherhood was as real for Blake as it (intermittently) is for us – 'the Great Harvest & Vintage of the Nations'. But until the Lamb is received by England

. . . Jerusalem is in that condition of ruin, captivity and abandonment described by Jeremiah in *Lamentations*.★ Once it was far different. When England was the spiritual Israel, it was a blessing to the whole Earth.

> London cover'd the whole Earth, England encompass'd the Nations,
> And all the Nations of the Earth were seen in Cities of Albion.

Jerusalem laments. We must remind ourselves that all this really goes on in the minds of men, in our own minds. The poet only makes it articulate. . . What, in fact, mitigates for Albion the rage of the Atlantic and constitutes a God-given promise for the future? Inspired art, Blake's own works. These works are given physical extension or material form: they are 'Spaces of Erin': they are also 'Sons and Daughters of Jerusalem', and 'Sons and Daughters of Los' because it is Los's hard work at his shaping furnaces that gives them their form as 'Spaces of Erin' . . .   Los is
> . . . the Spirit of Prophecy, the ever apparent Elias.
> Time is the mercy of Eternity; without Time's swiftness,
> Which is the swiftest of all things, all were eternal torment . . .
> Everyone is a fallen Son of the Spirit of Prophecy.

At the end of Blake's book the revelation of Jerusalem completes Los's integration. England awakes from death on Albion's breast – Albion awakes: 'into the Heavens he walked . . . speaking the Words of Eternity in Human Forms' –

> 'Do I sleep amidst danger to friends? O my Cities & Counties,
> Do you sleep! rouze up, rouze up! Eternal Death is abroad!'

★ & by myself – for the New Age – in 'Bank Holiday', (Latimer Press, '66)

So Albion spoke, & threw himself into the Furnaces of Affliction.
All was a Vision, all a Dream: the Furnaces became
Fountains of Living Waters flowing from the Humanity Divine.
And all the cities of Albion rose from their slumbers, and All
The Sons & Daughters of Albion on soft clouds Waking from Sleep.

Even so, 150 years later, do our intimations of 'the Divine
Appearance . . . the likeness & similitude of Los' recall us to
the timeless vocation of Jerusalem. Ginsberg is the type of
'fallen Son' compelled to spell it out in Time, to work, live –
and 'die only for poetry, that will save the world'. To tear off
the 'professional' poet's fancy-dress, all the masks of diplomacy,
and scream – 'Death to Van Gogh's Ear!' Naked but for
Elijah's mantle –

      Poet is Priest.
Money has reckoned the Soul of America
Congress broken thru to the precipice of Eternity
the President built a War Machine which will vomit and rear up
   Russia out of Kansas . . .
Einstein alive was mocked for his heavenly politics
Bertrand Russell driven from New York for getting laid
and the immortal Chaplin has been driven from our shores with the
   rose in his teeth . . .
I see nothing but bombs
I am not interested in preventing Asia from being Asia
and the governments of Russia and Asia will rise and fall but Asia and
   Russia will not fall
the government of America also will fall but how can America fall
I doubt if anyone will ever fall anymore except governments
fortunately all the governments will fall
the only ones which won't fall are the good ones
and the good ones don't yet exist
But they have to begin existing they exist in my poems
they exist in the death of the Russian and American governments
they exist in the death of Hart Crane & Mayakovsky .
Now is the time for prophecy without death as a consequence . . .

The vision 'I saw the best minds of my generation destroyed by madness / starving hysterical naked' set off the long-drawn-out *Howl* – to conjure back the lost insights of the minds destroyed – sacrificial lambs and scapegoats – beaten into King Lear's gone beatitude ("Tis the time's plague, when madmen lead the blind')★

★ It has become a matter of 'form' or 'principle' for British intellectuals to savage 'the Beats', however uncomprehendingly. Karl Miller, for example, in a gossipy review of 'Waiting for the End', asserted that the author – Leslie Fiedler – 'climbs the Ginsberg and plants there a flag marked with the word "Mad". A strange device, but it seems he is saying that madness is good... Like Whitman, (Ginsberg) is a patriot, a kind of filthy All-American Boy. He also serves'.

I wonder – to pause on the simplified level of this paraphrase – what it is Mr Miller finds so strange about the device. Can he deny that most current pressures in the cause of sanity – interpreted as nothing more or less than unquestioning adjustment to the social, moral and political norm – tend towards the inexorable suicide of humanity?

Let him consider Einstein's contention, that 'Religion without science is blind. Science without religion is lame.' – & Russell's, that 'The secret of happiness is to face the fact that the world is horrible, horrible, horrible – you must feel it deeply and not brush it aside . . .' – and then become happy. Let him remember the ultimately happy madness of Charlie Chaplin.

& then, let him consider *Waiting for Godot*. In the first act, Pozzo, the average sensual man of property & status is served, nourished and danced attendance by poor human suffering – in the starving deranged person of Lucky: whose impassioned, albeit broken outburst leaves no more doubt of the slave's spiritual superiority to his master than there is of his material dependence. At the end of his tether, Lucky wants nothing save to keep his dreadful job. . . On their second appearance – still tied by Pozzo's useless length of old rope – Lucky is dumb and his owner blind. In both scenes they're two figures any of the play's spectators might be – verging on the reversal and immanent destruction of every man-made force and value. & this is the god-forsaken stage our world is at – staggering to final curtains with a public bang here, a private whimper there: unless the money/power/armaments races can be called to a halt – the inane brutalism of our 'reality'-conditioning healed – madmens prophecies heard and 'a thousand blind windows' open –

– blasting at the mental uniforms on which conformist security rests ('unaccomodated man is . . . nothing more than such a poor, bare, forked animal'), and at the idols of totalitarian Babylon (read the Moloch choruses – out loud, if you dare) – with as much Old Testament intensity, music and symbology as falls into place ('Not purposely, I simply followed my Angel in the course of compositions'). This poet-priest's basic reverence stops short of exclusiveness, such as would bless none but Orthodox Jews. The dark inside river of his enlightenment would be drained away like the blood from Koshered meat. We're all one blood, whatever colour our several skins. Ginsberg addresses his independent observing conscience to that of all men, however unlearned – in the knowledge that all can become wise; & that in this Kali (destructive) Age the five senses remain 'the chief inlets of the Soul'. ★

'. . . I remembered the archetypal rhythm of Holy Holy Holy weeping in a bus on Kearney Street, and wrote most of it down in notebook there.' By this *Kedusha* (epiphany) 'everything that lives is holy':

It asks of us a kind of insanity to see in perspective a country, a planet going mad – to feel it deeply & not brush it aside – and retain one's own vision – 'an eye in the black cloud'; to see for what they are – and see through – the cupidity & chauvinism & genocide at the hub of power axes – Whitman's 'fabled Damned of nations' – the Kremlin Washington Westminster clubs – and survive *their* insanity; to see patriotism, understood as blind allegiance to governmental policies, is indeed the last refuge of a scoundrel – or a fool; see such 'elected' gods can only lead, from 'dull materialist vagaries about who should shoot who', to the third & probably the last world-war –

& still see the one government that lasts is the administrations of eternity, 'all Deities reside in the Human Breast'. If this be mad, Karl Miller, be glad for the method in it.

★ –See the interview with Ginsberg in the *Paris Review* of Spring 1966.

Holy! Holy! Holy!
Holy the groaning saxophone! Holy the bop apocalypse! Holy
    jazzbands marihuana hipsters peace & junk & drums!
. . . Holy the cafeterias filled with the millions! Holy the
    mysterious rivers of tears under the streets!

The free transposition of Judaic Litany with 'elastic' breath
emanations parallels those made by Negro R & B singers from
their spiritual sources, lifting our atomized awareness that
divinity does exist into total consciousness of its reality –
cleansing our senses – at the grass roots.

Poet-Priest* delves underground to the unknown centre of his
void, without losing heart, for bitterness to be transmuted.
Explores one drug after another, heightening awareness to the
outer reaches of cosmic bliss and terror: recognizing evil as a
state of experience through which the soul of man has to pass in
order to enter a nobler state, than the mere *Weltschmerz* – birth-
pangs of Good & Evil. To stare the hardest challenges of death
straight in the eye, and go on to greater heights – 'dying into
life' – kicking the drug-induced visionary *game*.

Thus has Ginsberg passed on, the Blakean way, from the
lowest depths of his being up, & out through the throbbing
voice-funnel – to embrace his poetic destiny, beyond the shades
of fate – exulting in the mental fight which discovers the pur-
pose of pain in self-knowledge, and perseveres – as Blake's
'Milton' does –

    . . . All that can be annihilated must be annihilated
    That the Children of Jerusalem may be saved from **slavery,**
    There is a Negation, and there is a Contrary:
    The Negation must be destroyed to redeem the Contraries.
    The Negation is the Spectre, the Reasoning power in man:
    This is a false body, an Incrustation over my Immortal

* uncomfortable term: choiceless position.

Spirit, a Selfhood which must be put off and annihilated always.
To cleanse the face of My Spirit by Self-examination,
To bathe in the Waters of Life, to wash off the Not Human,
I come in Self-annihilation and the grandeur of Inspiration.

– This presages the pattern of Ginsberg's movement towards satori and grace in *Kaddish*. Dismembered, unable to croon and mumble the stereotyped rites and orders in Shul, he regains his own innermost paradisiac source by wrestling with his ancestral God – making a sacred prayer of his own tears – for Naomi, and for the collective psyche – wrung from the shadow of her madhouse death:

... It leaps about me as I go out ... ... as I walk toward
        the Lower East Side – where you walked fifty years ago,
        little girl – from Russia, eating the first poisonous tomatoes
        of America – frightened on the dock ... toward what?
... Toward education marriage nervous breakdown, operation,
        teaching school, and learning to be mad, in a dream –
        What is this Life?

– A metaphor for that death of all the world we know, in whose shadow we daily walk, nightly dream –

Ai! Ai! we do worse! We are in a fix! And you're out, Death
        let you out, Death had the mercy, you're done with your
        century, done with God, done with the path thru it – Done
        with yourself at last – Pure – Back to the Babe dark before
        your Father, before us all – before the world –
... To go where? In that dark – that – in that God?   ...

Nameless, One Faced, Forever, beyond me, beginningless,
endless, Father in death. Though I am not there for this Prophecy,
I am unmarried, I'm hymnless, I'm heavenless, headless in bliss-
hood I would still adore Thee, Heaven after Death, only One
blessed in Nothingness, not light or darkness, Dayless Eternity –

... This is the end, the redemption from Wilderness, way for the
Wonderer, House sought for all, black handkerchief washed
clean by weeping – page beyond Psalm – Last change of mine
and Naomi – to God's perfect Darkness – Death, stay thy
phantoms!

Hard put to classify the mystic progression of *Kaddish* as either
'verse' or 'prose', A. Alvarez of the *Observer* concluded that it
can only be accepted as 'good psychotherapy' – in the absence
of an OK passport stamp such as 'stream of consciousness' now
seals Finnegan Unheard ...

Alvarez, like so many sideline commentators, seems to have
too much education – indoctrinated habits of imposing an
'objective' realism to censor the subconscious which, however
dormantly, registers our natural environment more meticu-
lously than prosaic words can tell. The painful efforts of
psychoanalysis only succeed in denoting reflex – reminding us
the soul will not submit to measurement. But it can be spiritually
sensed. Ginsberg's blithe acceptance of first intuitions in the
portrayal of his own soul, to the inclusion of socalled faults –
abnormality, 'indecency', 'filth' – gets considered critically,
intellectually, morally unpalatable. Superior salivations of the
cream of sense to be skimmed are bound to spoil the taste –
as was found by many would-be critics of Joyce:* In the

---

* My phrase is culled from Beckett's essay, 'Dante ... Bruno. Vico ...
Joyce' in *Our Exagmination* ... (Shakespeare & Co, Paris, 1929; Faber,
1961). W. C. Williams, in 'A Point for American Criticism' in the same
book, saw 'Joyce is breaking with a culture older than England's when
he goes into his greatest work. It is the spirit liberated to run through
everything, that makes him insist on unexpurgated lines and will not
brook the limitations which good taste would enforce. It is to break the
limitations, not to conform to the taste that his spirit runs. Naturally they
strain to drag him back. Here it is: he is going somewhere, they are
going nowhere. They are still looking back weighing (good enough); he
is going on, carrying what he needs and what he can. ... He is a
writer broken-hearted over the world (stick to literature as his chosen

synthesizing mind the wildest overflow of powerful emotions can coexist with 'high seriousness':

... Mind is shapely, Art is shapely. Meaning Mind practiced in spontaneity invents forms in its own image – gets to Last Thoughts. Loose ghosts wailing for body try to invade the bodies of living men. I hear ghostly Academies in Limbo screeching about Form –

(Note to Fantasy LP of *Howl* and *Kaddish*)

The exclusively mechanic directions of a technological millennium now conspire to overrule the individual struggle. In every society there are catalysts (amongst whom experimental scientists, architects & engineers) – and chemists. These days only the latter seem to turn out popularly and governmentally respected and (mis)understood as having definite things to say which they mean and communicate; and almost everything in our society gears them to do this perfectly – to no end other than spiritual, and then physical devastation. But not the artist's image, which celebrates with religious fervour – interlocked with the archetypal reality of man – disarming the subdivision commonplaces his radar-pawn would impose in the name of Progress.

Poet-Priest works on in the trust an inner knowing can be cultivated – *Amor vincit omnia*. In hearing the voice of the bard, we are invigorated by a symbolic exposition of the elusive integrating process – from psychosis to health – Temporal, to Eternal Man. That *Kaddish* reaches the ecstacy and catharsis to which it so powerfully builds – for poet, reader & listener alike – doesn't make it any the less a great poem. The depres-

---

symbol). Broken-hearted people do not bother about the place their tears are falling or the snot of their noses. ... The thing is, they (his critics) do not want to give up something, so they enlist psychology to save them. But under it they miss the clear, actually the miraculous, benefits of literature itself. A silent flower opening out of the dung they dote on. They miss Joyce blossoming pure white about their heads. They are *literary* critics ...'

sing point is that Alvarez and his readership are slaves of bad habit, stuck in the stocks – the stock-in-trade clichés and categories of urban literary sniping – incapable of hitting anywhere near Ginsberg, whose head is deep down the lion's mouth of madness – bringing death to life again, regenerating the womb of his own creation: achieving (as in his later *Wales Visitation*) an inevitability akin to that of Wordsworth's 'Immortality Ode' –

In the primal sympathy
Which having been must ever be;
In the soothing thoughts that spring
Out of human suffering;
In the faith that looks through death . . .

Ginsberg's bravery unlodes knowledge for us all – & the reaction of one of the most influential (Jewish) critics in Britain is to *complain* that it's come out in 'verse paragraphs – one can't call them lines any more' . . . Absurd how, in the heat of knocking the beatnik guru, all sense of literary history goes by the board (– I mean the almost identical use by Milton of blank verse paragraphs for rhythmic fluidity in *Paradise Lost* – 'the sense variously drawn out' – as opposed to end-stopt lines which 'bind and circumscribe the fancy'). For Ginsberg is as instrumental with density of image & syntax, elliptical suspension of main-verb sense relief, and overlapping & run-on phrases in piling up a cumulative resonance as Milton was in his massive organ structure.* Tho the American, as befits his matter, breaks

---

* & moving towards the poetic, if not yet the accomplishment, of Blake in *Jerusalem*: 'When this Verse was first dictated to me, I consider'd a Monotonous Cadence, like that used by Milton & Shakespeare & all writers of English Blank Verse, derived from the modern bondage of Rhyming, to be a necessary and indispensable part of Verse. But I soon found out that in the mouth of a true Orator such monotony was not only awkward, but as much a bondage as rhyme itself. I therefore have produced a variety in every line, both of cadences & number of syllables.

over a looser rhythmic base without the same weight of Lati
and more of messianic narrative expansions as per Whitman
Kerouac & Ray Charles blind blues-sobbing in the humid N
City air he was gulping and hollering out on the page:

... the long line now a variable stanzaic unit, measuring groups
related ideas – marking them – a method of notation. Ending wit
hymn in rhythm similar to the Synagogue death lament.

Milton entered the left foot of Blake, and Blake's voice car
into Ginsberg's day-dreaming head (reciting 'Ah Sun-flower
– which weeps pure poetry Van Gogh hears in heaven – ar
Alvarez cuts off his ear!   So Urizen strove with Milton

And took up water from the river Jordan, pouring on
To Milton's brain the icy fluid from his broad cold palm.

– Newton's 'sleep of reason' might be more helpful than th
parochial insensate reason – closer to the 'Sleep of Ulro' – b
of dehumanized abstract thought: which likewise muddies
and undermines the fertile ground of the same critic's Pengu
anthology, misleadingly promoted as *The New Poetry*.

For the oddest political un-reasons, every seer is rebuked
his time, dishonoured in his country. Blake knew – 'There a
States in which all visionary men are accounted mad men: su
are Greece & Rome' ...

Carlos Williams thought the fouling of Joyce's 'Work in Pr
gress' was because

Every word and every letter is studied and put into its fit place; the terri
numbers are reserved for the terrific parts, the mild & gentle for t
mild and gentle parts, and the prosaic for the inferior parts; all are nec
sary to each other. Poetry Fetter'd Fetters the Human Race. Nations a
Destroy'd or Flourish in proportion as Their Poetry, Painting and Mu
are Destroy'd or Flourish! The Primeval State of Man was Wisdo
Art and Science.'

. . . British criticism, like any other, is built upon the exigencies of the local literary structure and relates primarily thereto. Afterward it may turn to the appraisal of heterodox and foreign works. But if these are in nature disruptive to the first, the criticism will be found to be defensive, to preserve its origins –

& so the universities, & so the religions, & so the politics, & so the english death. But what Williams went on to say is less familiar:

. . . Forward is the new. It will not be blamed. It will not force itself into what amounts to paralysing restrictions. It cannot be correct. It hasn't time. It has that which is beyond measurement, which renders measurement a falsification, since the energy is showing itself as recrudescent, the measurement being the aftermath of each new outburst –

6

& just so did Edward Lucie-Smith seek to measure and disembody the Albert Hall Incarnation ('A Wild Night' – *Encounter*, August 1965):

. . . There was a triumph, which one might have wished otherwise. Adrian Mitchell, already well known for his political verses and for his powers as a reader of them, declaimed a clever but more than slightly smug poem about Viet Nam, and was rewarded with the biggest ovation of the evening. Yet there was an awareness that this was applause without catharsis, that the spectators were applauding the echo of their own sentiments, and willing themselves to be moved without truly being so – the stock response at work.

Inevitably, considering its size, it was something like a football or music crowd – largely made up of unpretentious connoisseurs, who knew, almost 'to a man', Mitchell had scored: a goal – a complete knock-out. They could divine from the very title ('To Whom It May Concern') what the reviewer is too obstinately obtuse to do – that here was a poem for everybody: its focal point of concern, resistance to the most lethal oppression everybody knew to be going on. It is Mitchell who adopts a consciantly critical attitude to reality – reality understood as what we *all* know – to be fact. Unanimous participation in such a poem is the concrete emblem of our common experience – so often withheld, pent-up, abused in public – being openly exposed and shared.

We are all, if we face the facts, inescapably implicated in that war: to face this together is to move towards doing something against it. Of course establishment journalists – to 'preserve the structure', maintain their positions, stay in business – have to fake ways of escaping the implication – gild flower-pots of reality.

Mitchell – who was a (radical) journalist for ten years – is as disenchanted as Günter Eich of 'decorating the slaughter-house with geraniums'. To answer the slur is not to say the poem needs any defence at all; but since it's printed heretofore, & since writers like Lucie-Smith, at least as much as writers like Mitchell and Eich, have conditioned the taste by which Penguin poems are savoured, it seems necessary to slam it home – that this kind of poem is good as it *does* good.

Mitchell freely admits its vulnerability in print, which often masks this kind of poem's drive to be resolved in terms of action; as that of the audience which so upset the *Encounter* critic – which it was, also, in the stage show *US*, and when Peter O'Toole thundered it over Trafalgar Square at the climax of the CND's Easter March from Aldermaston the same year. Public readings pave the course of that action, over against the closeted 'game-reserve' influences of Auden (who has tried to dismiss Blake as 'dotty', his later works as 'unreadable', & art and poetry as 'small beer' – tho this can't invalidate the luminous qualities of his own), & the stiff upper'd Schoolmen of 'Scrutiny' and 'the Movement' and 'the Group' and 'the Review'. The example of Mitchell guides younger poets away from that syndrome – which meant 'Most people ignore most poetry because most poetry ignores most people.' His own patently does not.

... The critics are scared ... because we are doing something very simple – trying to talk directly and honestly to people about the things which matter most to us – and the critics want complexity, they want exclusiveness. And it is easy to be complex and hard to take those parts of your vision which are most important and convey them, even if they are so simple that it's embarrassing to everyone who's even sniffed a university.

Verbal critics are going to get left farther & farther behind in understanding poets for whom the reading IS the thing – if they don't attend the readings. They may think they know what a poem ought to look like in a book, but invariably fail to dig – at first hearing, anyway, what's being done with the voice when a headstrong heart-song is held up to the light of its own extended experience.

Some excerpts from an interview Mitchell recorded for George MacBeth's broadcast, *A New Sound*, should help such novices.

MACBETH: ... a number of American poets – and Ginsberg's a good example, and Creeley is another very good example – have made their impact partly by words on the page, but usually much more so by reading them to people, and by their whole personalities of which the poems seem to be one part.

MITCHELL: Yes, well obviously I'm sympathetic with that. I find it less and less important to be published on the printed page. It has its uses but I think it's not very satisfying. In a poetry reading you can see exactly who you're talking to and you can hear what they're thinking to a certain extent; if things are going very well they respond by heckling you either positively or negatively. You're *there* – there's no question of sending this book away and hoping someone buys it ...

MACBETH: The *TLS* said 'there is a nucleus of poets who are starting to treat the writing and delivery of a poem as two stages in a single

process'. Does that seem to you a fair comment on what you
trying to do at the moment?

MITCHELL: Well, absolutely on what I was trying to do then. I w
starting to treat them as the same process and now more and mor
am treating them as the same process I hope.

MACBETH: Can I take you up on this word 'process', because I'm r
absolutely clear just what it means ... do you see the poem as s
in some way developing each time you read it aloud?

MITCHELL: Yes, I change poems when I read them aloud ... son
times ... not a lot – but it will change the way I feel about the po
and so it will change the way I read it. And so a poem is ne
finished until I stop wanting to read it – and then it's finished for me

MACBETH: You'd actually improvise names, for example, in relati
to a running perhaps social or political situation would you?

MITCHELL: Oh well, if it was possible to do that, yes ... and I
change poems, bring them up to date, all that kind of thing, a
write special verses on the train coming up to a town.

MACBETH: What I really meant was, while you are actually on yo
feet (YES) would you improvise spontaneously new ideas?

MITCHELL: Yes I do – both in the poems and between the poems
the time as well – they run into each other. I don't separate wha
try to do in between the poems from what I try and do in the
One of the best things about the readings is that there is no offic
censorship or criticism. The Lord Chamberlain never drops in a
the poetry critics rarely venture outside London. The audience
both censor and critic ... I suppose there is a kind of censorship tl
you put on yourself, but in the good readings there's no censorsl
at all; and I don't know of any place where writers can – work a
not be censored apart from those poetry readings in this count

MACBETH: You have two very powerful poems, one about Vietna
and another about Sir Alec Douglas Home before he was Sir A
Douglas Home – when he was Lord Home in fact. Now that o
has, you know, dated, and it doesn't seem to me that recently you'
written that kind of poem, and – if it comes to that, that down
date. But the Vietnam poem goes on – it retains its power beca
the war goes on. But isn't there some – if you like – issue o
similar kind directly affecting you as a – you know, British citize

MITCHELL: Well, peace and war affects me as a British citizen. And the way that war is going, it seems to me to influence Britain. I feel people in Britain are just as involved in the Vietnam war as people in America are. They've got less power to do anything about it.

MACBETH: They can't be drafted into an army to fight there though?

MITCHELL: No. They ca – not yet. And I don't think they'll have to fight in Vietnam. But they're going to have to fight a white man's war, which is what this whole thing is – what this war is. And – it's leading up to a global white man's war, eventually – maybe twenty, thirty years away if we're lucky . . .

Each time 'You Get Used To It' is heard audiences are re-awakened to the unabolished slavery in America – where the body of the nation has not, by all accounts, rid itself of the virus diagnosed by Ralph Ellison (in *Shadow And Act*, Secker & Warburg, 1967):

. . . the Negro was recognized as the human factor placed outside the democratic master plan, a human 'natural' resource who, so that white men could become more human, was elected to undergo a process of institutionalized dehumanization.

– Mitchell's blues voice expresses for us, as Jimmy Rushing's did for Ellison, 'a value and an attitude about the world for which our lives afforded no other definition'.

Voznesensky holds 'It is a poem's function / To be Shame's sensual organ'. Many oral poems are disposable: when they no longer stand up – when the cause for shame is redeemed, so are they – and only kept on paper as evidence of what's been overcome. And when this happens, no one is more relieved than the committed poet; we've no time or inclination to look *back* in anger. Mitchell would, I think, be glad to give up writing if it meant there were no need to read poems like these ever again. But the wars go on, censorship persists, bloodbaths 'escalate'. The whole subject of Vietnam has been hedged & distorted by Parliament, by the machinations of newspapers

and the prevailing hierarchies of opinion – certainly by CIA
sponsored *Encounter*.

Juicy Lucie's put-down X-rays the paralysis of the conven-
tional British sensibility to rear itself from what Burroughs
calls 'word lines', McLuhan 'linear culture', and hear the
words in time, like music – a time out of clock-time. Hung
on 'period' categories and prejudices – the disrepute into which
the celebrated 'public' poets of the thirties and Dylan Thomas
have fallen (the former partly by dint of their own deferential
retractions); on the 'idea' of poetry as remembered, dismem-
bered image – of slices of type – in the isolated armchair men-
tality; on verse as it's still too often taught – an exam-sloping
graph of scansion, rote & footnote; and on the decadent
chores of 'doing' a master-spirit a week at university, four
subjects o' weeklies thereafter; the fabricator of short notices
must needs read with the literal eyes of theory – respond only to
the uncustomary, unwelcome sound of a huge London
audience provoked to uproar by a poem – and not to the sound
of the poem itself. The best part of 7,000 listeners knew, what
Yvor Winters has deduced, that

... the mind's ear can be trained only by way of the other (i.e. the
physical ear), and the matter, practically considered, comes inescapably
back to the reading of poetry aloud.

Lucie-Smith's ear must be presumed as null as that of Alvarez:
how, otherwise, could he have missed the rhythm of the whole
poem – the loud unmistakeable noise it made – the staccato
syncopated tone, pitch and thinking-feeling phrasing Mitchell
gave it specifically for that internationalist assembly: the sheer
technique, of *prosody*, as defined by Pound – 'the articulation of
the total *sound* of the poem'.   The total sound is, in this case, an
ironic sound. Not the sometimes complacently civilized irony
of Eliot, or MacBeth's verse; a more primitive kind, as was
quite obvious to all but the most hidebound receptivity – an

irony savagely directed *against* the speaker of the poem – the 'don't want to know' type of speaker. Though the poem retains compassion for him too, acknowledging it could be – at unwatchful moments is – himself, anyone. This is how it is, Mitchell says – the reverse of smugly. He makes no pretence of offering political answers – simply snarls for real decency, intelligence, imagination.

The truth hurts, he says – & gradates instantly from the stripped metaphor of his opening statement to the ironic one of 'stick my legs in plaster / Tell me lies about Vietnam'. Our arms factories and missile bases and bomb shelters provide crutches: wearing them, it's more comforting to forget it is they – the protagonists of *realpolitik*, Einstein's 'Science without religion' – who've cut off our legs. The government recommends specs on National Health, which 'correct' our vision – from seeing it's the hand-me-down consolations of patriotic faith, the superficial 'Religion without science' (but 'God on our side') – that blinded us in the first place.

The welfare state inures us against feeling the pain of others – up to a point. Most of the systematically maimed, butchered and burning flesh is thousands of miles away. We may be mentally ravaged, but we generally manage to appear well dressed in secure jobs enjoying secure credit in securely stabilized socio-economic leagues – taking pride in our national history & esteem 'abroad', our motor cars, banks, sportsmen, clowns – and if all this is temporarily disturbed by an 'atrocity picture' we can switch off, rush out, roam the cities and countryside, gobble oodles of multi-coursed meals a day, bask in each other's reassuringly cosy homes & farms & views & whisky & women galore.

Mitchell spits out his confession – for all to confess – admit the price of all this: that the Vietnamese have only desolation and rape and death by knife and fire. The price is lies – lies tailor-made for public wear without tears – about negroes in South

Africa (from which Mitchell has been barred) and Rhodesia, about 'balance of terror' – lies about Spam and lies about napalm – all told and believed in the name of 'the economy' and 'diplomacy', of 'education' and of 'justice' – the Organization Man's doomed stereo-typed gunfire – his premium predigested pap, his pulp, his news of the world – for the Sunday people want breadlines – security – furrowed tanklines & sex in the headlines.   & the overfed spectators want confirmation of their smuggery, pseudo-intellectual scented merde . . .

The hordes that crowded out Albert Hall were hungry – for something else. Most of them had probably been to more readings than most critics, but they'd never been treated to such a banquet as this. Yes, they were in high spirits, partly cheering themselves – having achieved such a concentrated identification, unity – through the 'common loneliness', gutburst therapy of Mitchell's ballad. But this unity was in *opposition* to the stock response – the bovine acceptance by the British public at large of Wilson's proposition, that we 'owe it' to America, to support her wars.

This particular British public applauded its soothsayer, as a revolutionary Hungarian one might applaud Gyula Ilyès's 'Bartok', which ends (by my translation) –

. . . Work, good doctor, never soporific,
work on with the fingers of your music
    touching our soul,
        touch even
to the darkest roots of horror.
How strange, how blissful a remedy you bring us
    when your voice, and the taut strings of your nerves,
speaks the agony which would burst from us all, but cannot
    – for we are born to silence of heart!

– And yet, as these mammoth occasions have shown, we will *not* be censored, will not accept the diet of lies. Our tongues gasp, lust for truth – the whole truth, to be spoken out in the open. None the less true, in regard to Vietnam, tho we already know: with Hugh Jenkins – one of the few MPs who does tell it publicly –

... the truth is that the American government has dehumanized itself towards Vietnam as the Germans dehumanized themselves towards the Jews, and all of us who countenance this, going about our daily tasks and averting our minds from the reality, are as guilty as were the German people in the last war.

The British government and in particular the Prime Minister and Foreign Secretary are infected by this dehumanization, for they do not permit themselves to condemn the burning of children, and they answer questions by saying, in effect, that to become human, to plead with the Americans for mercy towards the children of Vietnam would be to lessen their standing with this monstrous government and so handicap them in their search for peace. They add that the other side is also killing people and they would like it all to end. The Tories call 'Hear, hear' and that is the end of that. In the meeting of the Parliamentary Labour Party, as has been reported, I asked the Prime Minister to agree that the resumption of the bombing was a mistake. He replied by saying that it was inevitable. No doubt that was said about the killing of the Jews, the dropping of the atom bomb and the slaughter of Dresden, but none of these things was really inevitable. The mass killing of defenceless human beings only becomes inevitable because men shut themselves off from feeling what is being done for fear that they should go mad. In that fear they deprive themselves of the pity which alone can save mankind from man.

(*New Statesman*, February, 1966)

7

      Today, it came to me. How you
      My friends, who write, who draw
      And carve, friends who make pictures,
      Plays, finger delicate instruments,
      Compose, or fake, or criticize – how

In the oncoming megaton bombardments,
All you stand for will be gone,
Like an arrow into hell.

. . . It is true.
They will say you are fools
Who know nothing of politics.
Women and artists must keep out of politics.
. . . They will suggest –
Politely, politely – your hair
Is too long for sanity.
Even though you are bald with worry.
. . . They will,
With their reason,
Prove your unreasonableness.
Though you are dying from rationality.

They will do all in their power,
And their power is great,
To shut you up –

All of this, from 'To My Fellow Artists' by Christopher
Logue, has more or less happened. Mitchell recalls that Logue,
in 1957

. . . was challenging poets to react to nuclear warfare, inviting us to
fight against our rulers. I remember at the time thinking – well, I
am reacting in my poems. Then I thought – and nobody knows it.

Spelling out direct intuitions – on a private and a political level,
and really grooving in with music, are two elements the British
activity since that time has been able to teach American poets –
& politicians and musicians everywhere.

The extremes of political orientation as formalized by Logue
& Mitchell owe something to Brecht & to Russian precedents,
but their main impulse is firmly rooted in the indigenous tradi-
tions of radical dissension. Jerusalem was never utterly lost here

in the sense of Liberty – but it slid into abuse by the very 'toler-
ance' – of 'non-conformism', 'eccentricity' – all questioning
motions dully incorporated into the insular conserving systems.
The opponents of Jerusalem – in the sense of building, realizing
a visionary society – are checked by this responsible emancipa-
tion of public speech. That which has lain dormant awakes – &
England has been a heavy sleeper – assumes the conscious,
vertical level – in meditation, prophecy, protest and song: a
living depth, the depth of a waking man – tho sometimes like
Ginsberg's 'best minds' he 'stand before you speechless and
intelligent and shaking with shame'.

Mercifully, in the new underground exchanges, he's more
often highly articulate – being more confident, nowadays, that
he has an audience that cares. As Mitchell was, in his speech-
poem for the July '67 'Legalize Pot' rally in Hyde Park (– most
of the thousands of participants were wearing or carrying
flowers):

> ... These flowers are for love.
> Good. That seems to be what we're alive for.
> But is it a vague gas of love
> Which evaporates before it touches another human being
> Or is it a love that works?
> A love so strong that it can free
> A prisoner in Spain or Russia?
> A love so bright that it can illuminate forever
> The hideous darkness of the African sky?
> A love so loud that it can shout BE FREE
> To the imprisoned states of South America?
> A love so explosive that its tremors
> Will shake out of the sky
> The bombers which at this minute
> Are murdering Hanoi?
> A love so hot that it can melt the armaments
> Before they melt the entire country of Vietnam
> And maybe the inflammable sea

The inflammable earth
The inflammable sky
And the inflammable people of the earth.
Or is it so small a love
That it has no more chance of changing the world
Than a poppy seed planted under the concrete floor
Of a nuclear power station?

It must become a love huge enough
To tear down all the offices
Where poverty, hunger, imprisonment and war are planned.
It must become a love intelligent and vast enough
To build Jerusalem, a million Jerusalems,
      A world more loving
Than our most astonishing visions.

Disinterred from the basements of our personalities, through the accumulation of meetings & travels & readings & talks & publications, the awakening of muses and conscience has mounted – 'heart in heart, and hand in hand'. Ten years ago only a few people seemed to be concerned, writing chiefly *about* verse: now so many more are effectively talking – poetry itself – & listening, to one another – thinking, whispering, playing, shouting, drawing, painting, printing, praying, singing and dancing and acting it out: their recaptured birth-right.

Newcomers flourish amid a lavish diversity of standpoints. Melomantic & manic sound-poets by turns entertain and harangue the lumpen Social Security queues: & a gallery, hoarding, building site or shopping centre across the street may house films, prints, LPs, graffitti and sculptures of the concrete corps, or more.

Harwood (experimenting years ago with a new objectivism: 'poetry today should not just wail, but really examine the world around us') and Hollo (usually well ahead of 'the difficulties in diction . . . our British poets seem to be having. It is as if the real *world* they, we, are living in is only slowly beginning to dawn on them') have instigated many changes during their many phases – enriched by continental and american examples without merely aping them.

Oram launches the mind into space:

. . . . The High Dive

. . . the pull from my passing

reforms the whole.

The 'artist', if he consciously chooses not to 'dive deeper', is (in rearranging existing experience-patterns) refusing to enter the unknown . . . & is therefore anti-religious. . . There is a tremendous temptation to 'live' in another's pattern, & try to improve upon it; but we can see that this adjusting of memory patterns is really aimed at distracting the soul from returning to its source.

('Clouds and Cages' – unpublished)

& Dave Cunliffe looks east:

– It is the yogic path I follow. . . I see Mantric poetry as an underground communications network to and from the centre of things. True poet a magic sacred Word Bodhisatva directing a beautiful underground system of deliverance of all who exist. That is why I feel the poet should be revolutionary, illuminated, an advanced adept/ initiate of Love and not involved in power-abuse (politics, exploitation, authority), War Machine Spectres, fleshmeat eating of sentient beings or any other hangups of embryonic humanity. – This is war on *all* fronts. We are *all* brothers under the skin. Freedom for *all*. – Engage the Self at all levels, expand, transcend. Walk on. Beyond thought, time, forever.

('The Total Revolution', *Resurgence* 7, 1967)

Yeats carried the classic baton of myth-making into this century; many of the new poets are more intent on pursuing their own invented or emergent mythology – living symbolically. Others retain detachment: Crozier, Evans, Finlay, Fisher,

Guest, Torrance and Turnbull employ cooler aesthetic
approaches.

Dom Silvester Houédard suggests –

EITHER you see the modern movement as happening to american
poetry (whether written in GB or USA) OR you see it as happening
to english poetry (whether written in USA or GB); in 1st case you
restrict english poetry to victorian-georgian-neoelizabethan: in 2nd
case you see wild zigzag life linking well f i (Whitman) Pound Stein
Sitwell Cummings Eliot Auden Williams Spender Olson Ginsberg
Corso Horovitz Heliczer Hollo & the jazzpoetry of now ...
poetry life is openness to ALL influences that influence language/life so
english poetry must feel all its fringe developments (late silver low
dog pidgin) specially mad african & not just american: feel too the
french stances to reality & german concern with ordering noise ...
the jazz poems (& all poems breathing today) are on the way to
equalizing reader/author: giving the reader not the cage with a dead
poem in it but the openness that lets the reader get the immediacy the
shared experience of CREATING the poem: they're not forcing
readers/hearers into guest positions but getting him to take the host
attitude. Author talks to reader as though he were the moi image of
the je (Burroughs loss-of-outline: jazz immediacy: double innerness
at Marienbad ...

('Beat & Afterbeat', *Aylesford Review*, Summer, 1963)

Nearly all the poets in this book make it their business to keep
up with each other's work – always 'the next job' to appreciate,
sometimes emulate (not the mockery of reviews). The Ameri-
can critic M. L. Rosenthal finds it

... hard to believe that out of so much ferment, so many readings, so
much response to the outside world's doings, the English are not on
the verge of a brilliant new period

– the return of Albion's golden age?

The most concentrated flashpoint comes round again and
again in wonderment at the widespread distillations of lyric
essence – secret & fanfared – whose imaginative objectives are

constantly kept moving higher and higher. The ballads and fairy tales and satires of Donovan, Bert Jansch, Stan Kelly, Leon Rosselson, Alasdair Clayre, the Incredible String Band, & the ululating beat groups, even unto the Beatles and Stones, often reflect virtues picked up from the 'straight' poets, play mechanic to the propellors – pilots – inventors of audibly supersonic spacecraft.

Patten's generation – younger than the new Hiroshima – plays – is – poetic Adam. A street-urchin rolling in moss that presses up sharp shoots between the pavement-blocks to joy with Blake's Adam Kadmon, reborn each day with the entire universe – all its elements & toys & constellations at his disposal – whose answer to all this is to sing his voyage through it, as sensuously as he can.

... I'm amazed I'm on this, this city with winds and grass blowing through, and it's like being on a planet, and this planet is in this universe, and the clouds are going past me. . . . It's a fantastic feeling. I'm trying to get this into my poems. Mainly lyric, the hard lyric.

We're weaving our own several embroideries (without 'living in another's pattern') on the sublime nuclear bing-bang loom inherited from Corso and Voznesensky and Kops, who blow up the bomb in the best blast blessible – outlining its look & boom in haphazard mosaics of words which locate the explosions in their psyche, to express them – creatively. Where Eliot revived the 'dissociation of sensibility', and the Surrealists by juxtaposing two objects revealed each more clearly itself, the *act* of juxtaposition is now zoomed forth – kaleidoscoped – in a new unified sensibility.

Corso was perhaps the first to show (through the *bright* jigsaw a bomb *does* charge – 'budger of history/brake of time . . . lyre and tuba together joined' – *in imagination*) that we can't write only in fear – as tho the atom were the monster, it and not ourselves defined the power. & let fly a hymn from his pen – 'neither for or against the bomb' says Ginsberg, 'it just reduces the bomb to insignificance because the poem is greater than the bomb'. Modern man must improvise on his inventions if he's not to be enslaved by them – subliminally reduced to a button-pushing computer's dummy.

Another astral spur to the dynamic pace set in this territory – constructing firebirds of the word to fit man for the moon & stellar worlds in wait, and contain the technologic mutations now at hand to transport our bodies – is Fainlight's apotheoses of lyricism. At Albert Hall (having served a thoroughgoing apprenticeship in New York) he dedicated his 'Larksong' specifically to English poets – to rouse up whole galaxies of song – the poem a machine to outlive the most insolent raids on inner and outer space, the violent cosmic vicissitudes that may be to come, with the conviction they'll be finally integrated in the planet-chanting of it:

Fresh wildernesses!
Resurrected from the raw-broken concrete at the airfield's edge.
Where, mounting from the coursing grasses, a lark's
Fistful of blood and feathers flings
Its song into the teeth of the wind
Then drops back broken.

O bursting minstrel heart pounding
Amidst those thrashing grasses, yet but once more rise,
Climb, oh shine out emblematically against
That ceaseless silver soaring and settling.

Yea, even to where the giant rocket-ship is standing
Balanced upon its own exhaust-blast terrible,
O sing, ecstatic; unshaken by
That heart-shaking, cathartic roar.

8

Atomic Adams, visibly erupting instead of falling, father the lineaments of a new renaissance personality – athwart the Philistine & Pharisee critics alike, dead hands of repressive control – towards Blake's 'Universal Poetic Genius' and Jung's 'Collective Unconscious'.

In America, Holland, Paris, Germany and Scandinavia this has been socialized in the formation of actual underground communities in which diggers, hippies and unclassifiable deviants live as virtually autonomous tribes, with food & clothing, shelter & beds, families & frenzies & arts democratically shared. The undergrounds here have thus far found rather less to react against and dispose themselves in looser-knit strands of activation – often quite positively occupied within existing local structures as well as the long-wave interzones. Group projects pile up – Roundhouse conferences – pilgrimages to Glastonbury – the 'jungle republic' of Ladbroke Grove – the Anti-university in Shoreditch – & the Covent Garden *International Times*/Middle Earth/Arts Laboratory complex (tho this has occasionally fallen prey to the 'swinging London' Babylon of hucksters, fixers and double-agents).

And whilst most of us retain the traditional patterns of family-friend-lover-small group living, Albion's children are strongly in evidence all over the country and – most colourfully & plentifully – all over London, at work and play in their own gardens of love, where only 'Thou Shalt Not' is taboo – in an atmosphere of finer awareness, radiating a *sense* of community & a more open, humane and practical way of life – of which much of this Miscellany is the best symbolic expression.

In songs of innocence & experience as sensitive to the calculated threats to contemporary life as Blake's were – catching up and redirecting rays from the talented makers of underground movies & posters & music & environments – we're cleansing language of the perversions wished on it by Admass 'brainwashers', ghost writers, statesmen of the nations. Often – as in Ginsberg's 'Wichita Vortex Sutra' college – transcribing and incorporating the rusty war-jingles & Newspeak prevarications of politicians (*overkill* for 'murder') with our own restoration of linguistic and moral value. Spreading an aesthetic wing for the daily more effectual changes wrought by students – & teachers – all over; of whom many will surely be in the 'running' of such countries as last out to, well – 1984?

Brown has a poem proposing that more living arts centres, revolutionary seminars & kibbutzim be set up, to accommodate the wide potential of energies now being spawned:

They should really have farms
for poets poets should be like cows
milked twice a day
and those that don't produce should be eaten . . .

The snag is, of course, that where something like this arrange-ment already exists, as in Russia, it's sometimes those that do produce who get eaten – because their milk of human kindness doesn't meet the policy requirements of the marketing board commissars. Viz. – the indictment and exile of Joseph Brodsky as a 'workshy element' and 'dangerous parasite' for working at nothing but his poetry and translations; the vicious banishment of Russia's Ginsburg and his underground friends;★ and the censorship by Khruschev of the punchlines of Yevtushenko's 'Babiy Yar' – probably his most valid polemical verses – in

★ In 1959 Alexander Ginsburg had the idea of putting loose typescripts together & produced two issues of the first widely distributed under-ground magazine – *The Syntax* – himself ('Samizdat' = Self-publisher, i.e. without sanction of the Party censor); after which he disappeared for two years. But more than a dozen others rose up in its wake – above all, the *Phoenix 66* (containing such lines as Stefanov's – 'Russia, I have of you/ A double image in my heart;/Are you a song or a howl,/Are you a bird or a bitch?/Are you a song or a howl?/Are you immortality or putrefac-tion?'), whose editor Galanskov has just been condemned to seven years behind the barbed wire. Ginsburg, too, will now spend another five years in a labour camp, for having collated the secret transcript of the Siny-avsky-Daniel trial – news of which has consequently sped round the world.

which he faced the challenge of the unabating anti-Semitism in his country, & the emptiness at the ravine where some 70,000 Jews were massacred by the Nazis – to cry out

> Let the Internationale
> > thunder
> when the last anti-semite on earth
> is buried forever.
> In my blood there is no Jewish blood.
> In their callous rage all anti-semites
> must hate me now
> > as if I were a Jew.
> And for that reason
> > I am a true Russian!

– Tho in the end he's called to cry, not so much for Russia – and surely not a Russia which silences his truth – as in the name of poetry.

Professor Leavis said

. . . Poetry matters because of the kind of poet who is more alive than most people, more alive in his own age. He is, as it were, the most conscious point of the race in his time.

And the race which matters most is not white or Russian or American or Chinese or British or Jewish or Hungarian or Afro-Asian or Black – still less any of the careering rat-races – but that of all mankind, chosen by birth in this age to shoulder the burdens of world citizenship. By the legislature of poetry, creeds & charters & patriotic loyalties are no substitute for self-examination; but in their conviction that the race is still worth running (& race memory depends on race futurity), nearly all living poets are believers, with Yevtushenko – 'My religion is a belief in man!'   For my part –

> When I was two
> the Nazis came –
> we had to flee

For that accident of birth it was Fight the good fight
– You're a Jerry, they said at school, &
– You're a Jew – You go to Shul –

'Hardpunch Horofist' I became & fought
for that same different me
not for jolly Germany, not the Chosen race
for daily face to face I saw – each one of us
chosen for the human race

Why fight! – if fight, fight for that – for you
and you and her and he
– fight for *all* humanity . . .

– These lines from my lay sermon 'For Modern Man' (1914–1964, RIP) read at Albert Hall were scorned by Lucie-Smith as in 'the shade of Ella Wheeler Wilcox': but I've never read the lady: Blake, Edward, shades of Albion rising – 'giving himself For the Nations' –

In my Exchanges every Land
Shall walk, & mine in every Land,
Mutual shall build Jerusalem . . .

Would-be customs officials of these continuing exchanges will have to slough their Spectre (intellectual power divorced from the imagination). In so far as we enjoy more of the privileges of civilized freedom in Britain, to be simply poets and men, there's that much more responsibility – to do more – not simply barricade a fairest isle unto ourselves.

Thus did Ted Hughes – drawing on the brio of the Albert Hall congresses, and bringing to corporeal life his far-reaching 'Modern Poetry in Translation' circulars – organize a 'Poetry International '67' on the South Bank, announcing

. . . poets from nine different countries will take part. The idea for such a gathering was suggested by the great and growing public for poetry which is making itself felt in London just as surely as in Moscow and New York. However rootedly-national in detail it may be,

poetry is less and less the prisoner of its own language. It is beginning to represent, as an ambassador, something far greater than itself. . .
The idea of global unity is not new, but the absolute necessity of it has only just arrived, like a sudden radical alteration of the sun, and we shall have to adapt or disappear. If the various nations are ever to make a working synthesis of their ferocious contradictions, the plan of it and the temper of it will be created in spirit before it can be formulated or accepted in political fact. And it is in poetry that we can refresh our hope that such a unity is occupying people's imaginations everywhere, since poetry is the voice of spirit and imagination and all that is potential, as well as of the healing benevolence that used to be the privilege of the gods.

Ginsberg is accused of becoming an Establishment – good – if his inspiration can be absorbed, as it was at this state-sponsored meeting, without being compromised. If underground & overhead can be welded by the poetic state ('one by one and four by four'), nationalistic states might drop out for real – hallowing *this* world's space for the 'social place for the soul to exist' – every man a special kind of artist – & no call for underground *resistance* any more.

But if (like Yevtushenko, after being exported as a wonder boy of post-Stalinism, withdrawn from circulation because – like Voznesensky – he will not be 'directed') our underdogs can be strangled to heel by frustrate owners (tied to their own possessiveness); if the hippie movement eventually rings in nothing more than the jukebox concord of Carnaby St & Tin Pan Alley; if festivals like Hughes's have to be qualified, in utilizing the facilities of the governing literary bureaucracy, by restricting themselves to poetry of which that bureaucracy can entirely approve – and yet be ostracized by the Russians; then revolution only comes full circle to reassert the triumph of warheads and crypto-satanic mills of power & profit & failure scraping the charter'd skies.

The achievement of the beats in speaking through with their

poetry intact to all walks of american life was besmutted – in the early (missionary) years – by the populist chicaneries of *Time – Life*, the 'full shmeer'-type treatments we forbore from a London gutter-press investigator (to be awarded gratuitously vindictive brickbats in his compilation 'Generation X'). Unsolicited publicity is a continual bugbear. But some of the younger British poet-readers, & wives & friends, are planning a new kind of booking agency, tentatively called 'Poetry in Motion'. So my dream of a beaming bush telegraph transporting bards over land, sea & air in a wondrously painted chariot of fire may yet come true – subsisting on our own poetic aether beyond acknowledged legislators.

Meanwhile the magnificent readings in Moscow's Mayakovsky Square on Poetry Day have not revived since the Khruschev purges. New books of Russian verse are none the less ravenously devoured – sometimes sold out in advance editions of a million copies. There's obviously an enormous appetite for poetry on the part of the newly literate audiences there, and in other East European countries which are said to convene readings on the grand scale: countries where it has long been relished, as it is just beginning to be again nearly everywhere on earth, by a popular and not an elite concensus, for the highest form of literature – the fountainhead

– from which we stream, taking ever newer departures – however these may lead us on, back and round to perennial sources. Moving – eternally toward the light – communion, vision, delight – to combat the darkness, clear the shadows between motion and act, emotion and response – to give functioning local habitation in the middle of society to the art which belongs to all people: remaking languages round which the new global tribes can settle – purifying the dialects of the world:

Without encroaching on that 'sullen craft' so pure it can only be practised 'where men and mountains meet'; which perforce remains hermetic – carved on the rock, sealed in the book, blessed by the Chariot of Contemplative Thought.

Yet if the prophet of Jerusalem were on his ancient feet I don't doubt but he'd be sending more men to higher mountains by singing his songs and blowing his ever present mind of prophecy to the many who rejoice to hear today.

> Each Man is in his Spectre's power
> Untill the arrival of that hour,
> When his humanity awake
> And cast his own Spectre into the Lake.
>
> And there to Eternity aspire
> The selfhood in a flame of fire
> Till then the Lamb of God . . .

– The unfinished work of Blake – of this unfinished poem – is ours to carry on. The legacy of the whole man.

MICHAEL HOROVITZ
April 1968

For further information on these matters *See:*

PETE BROWN, 'A Report on the Edinburgh Poets' Conference', *Granta*, 1240, Cambridge, 28 November 1964. 'Americans in Albion' *Circuit 2*, Cambridge, 1966

ALISDAIR CLAYRE, 'Words for Music', *TLS*, 1 February 1968

DAVE CUNLIFFE and TINA MORRIS (ed), 'The New British Poetry', *Poetmeat 8*, Blackburn, 1964

HARRY FAINLIGHT, 'Reverse Adam', *International Times*, December 1967

LAWRENCE FERLINGHETTI, ALLEN GINSBERG, and GREGORY CORSO, *Penguin Modern Poets 5*, 1963

PETER FRYER, 'A Map of the Underground', *Encounter*, October 1967

RICHARD GILBERT, 'The Emergence of the London Underground, *Town*, March 1967

ADRIAN HENRI, ROGER MCGOUGH, and BRIAN PATTEN, *Penguin Modern Poets 10*, 1967

ANSELM HOLLO (ed), *Jazz Poems*, Vista Books, London, 1962
'Fake It New', *Evergreen Review 26*, 1963
(ed), 'New Sounds in British Poetry', *Evergreen 38*, 1965

MICHAEL HOROVITZ, 'The Blake Renaissance', *Oxford Opinion*, Spring 1958
'Way Out', *New Departures 1*, Oxford, Summer 1959
'Points of Departure', *New Departures 2–3*, London, 1960
'The Poetry', Live New Departures at St Pancras Town Hall Programme, London, 1961
'News About Time', *New Departures 4*, London, Spring, 1963
'Jazz & Poetry', *Jazz News and Review*, 16 May 1963
'Live New Departures', Festival of Poetry at the Royal Court Theatre Booklet, Poetry Book Society, Summer 1963
(ed), 'New Poetry, New Jazz', Live New Departures at St Pancras Town Hall Programme, Spring 1964
'A Circle for the Square World', *The Times Literary Supplement* 'Changing Guard' issue, 4 August 1964
monthly programme notes for Live New Departures in the ICA *Bulletins* from December 1964 to October 1966, especially

'Lyres that Tell the Truth', December 1965

'Poets & Their Audience', *New Society*, 6 June 1965

'Stirring Times', letter about the Albert Hall reading in *TLS*, 2 September 1965

'On the Beat with Gregory Corso', *Penthouse,* Volume 1 No. 8, London, 1965

'Poets or PROs', debate with John Horder, *Ambit* 27, 1965

'Leaves . . . from a Book of Changes', for Better Books one-man show, December 1965/January 1966

'Poetry in Motion', *Books* (journal of the National Book League), Poetry Number, Summer 1967

(ed), 'Brave New Departures Revisited' programme, at All Saints Hall, London, WII, 15 December 1968

'Nova – Come on!' – Open Letter to *International Times* (48), January 1969

ALAN JACKSON, JEFF NUTTALL, and WILLIAM WANTLING, *Penguin Modern Poets* 12

BOB LEESON, 'They bring poetry direct to the people', *Morning Star*, 25 October 1968

ADRIAN MITCHELL, 'Poetry is Bursting out of its Ghetto', *Morning Star*, 6 July 1967

Guide to the Underground, *Guardian*, 12 October 1967

(ed – with twelve other poets) *Poetry in Motion* poet-readers' agency brochure, London, September 1968

JEFF NUTTAL, *Bomb Culture,* MacGibbon & Kee, 1968

IRIS ORTON, pamphlets *With Music in Mind & Beyond Catharsis,* Samizdat, London & Stockholm, 1959 and 1966

ALAN RIDDELL, 'A Chair Flies in Berners St', *Scene 8*, London, 1963

PETE ROCHE (ed), *The New Love Poetry*, Corgi Books, London, 1967

DAVID SLADEN, 'Credo', *New Departures* 1, Oxford, Summer 1959

FELIKS TOPOLSKI, Topolski's Chronicle on the Albert Hall reading, London, Autumn 1965

DAVID WIDGERY, 'The Arts Council – a counter-plan', U-magazine special (12), London, Autumn 1966

PETER WHITEHEAD's Book of the film, *Wholly Communion,* Lorrimer Publishing 66

Acknowledgements

For permission to reprint poems in copyright, thanks are due to the following:

For PETER ARMSTRONG: to the author and View Publications for poems from *28 Poems*, 1966. For PETE BROWN: to Fulcrum Press for poems from *Let em roll Kafka*, 1969 and *Selected Poems*, 1969. For BARRY COLE: to the author and to Methuen & Co. Ltd, for the poem 'Reported Missing' from *Moonsearch*, 1968 for 'The Question'. For PAUL EVANS: to Fulcrum Press for poems from *Love Heat*, 1969. For IAN HAMILTON FINLAY: to the author, to New Directions for poems from *New Directions in Prose & Poetry*, 20 © 1968 by New Directions Publishing Corporation, and to Fulcrum Press for poems from *The Dancers Inherit the Party*, 1969. For ROY FISHER: to Migrant Press for poems from *City*, 1960, to Tarasque Press for poems from *Ten Interiors with Various Figures*, 1966, and to Fulcrum Press for poems from *Collected Poems*, 1969. For HARRY GUEST: to the author and Anvil Press Poetry for poems from *Arrangements* © 1968 and to Outposts Publications for a poem from *A Different Darkness* and for the poem *Private View*. For LEE HARWOOD: to Fulcrum Press for poems from *The White Room*, 1969 and *Landscapes*, 1969, and to Angel Hair for poems from *The Man with Blue Eyes*, 1967. For SPIKE HAWKINS: to Fulcrum Press for poems from *The Lost Fire Brigade*, 1968, and to Tarasque Press for poems from *Spike Hawkins Poems*, 1965. For ANSELM HOLLO: to Migrant Press for poems from *& it is a Song*, 1965 © Anselm Hollo, to Turret Books for poems from *The Man in the Treetop Hat*, 1968 © Anselm Hollo, and to Ambit Books for poems from *Faces and Forms*, 1965 © Anselm Hollo. For FRANCES HOROVITZ: to St Albert's Press for poems from *Poems*, 1967. For JOHN JAMES: to the Ferry Press for poems from *Mm – Ah Yes*, 1967. For BERNARD KOPS: to Scorpion Press for poems from *Erika, I Want to Read You Something*, 1967. For HERBERT LOMAS: to Mandarin

Books for *Chimpanzees Are Blameless Creatures*. For TOM MCGRATH:
to Ambit Books for poems from *My Love Stop Rain Stop*, 1969. For
ADRIAN MITCHELL: to the author and Jonathan Cape Ltd, for
poems from *Poems*, 1964, and to Cape Goliard for poems from *Out
Loud*, 1968. For EDWIN MORGAN: to Edinburgh University Press
for poems from *The Second Life*, 1968. For PHILIP O'CONNOR: to
Jonathan Cape Ltd, for the poem from *Selected Poems 1936–1966*,
1968. For TOM PICKARD: to Fulcrum Press for poems from *High on
the Walls*, 1967. For PAUL POTTS: to the author and Eyre and
Spottiswoode Ltd, for 48 lines from *Dante Called You Beatrice*, 1961.
For TOM RAWORTH: to Goliard Press for poems from *The Relation
Ship*, 1966, to Trigram Press for poems from *The Big Green Day* and
to Fulcrum Press for poems from *Selected Poems*, 1969. For BARRY
TEBB: to the author and Poet & Printer for a poem from *The
Quarrel with Ourselves*, 1966. For CHRIS TORRANCE: to the Ferry
Press for poems from *Green, Orange, Purple, Red*, 1968. For GAEL
TURNBULL: to the author and Cape Goliard Press for poems from
A Trampoline, 1968.

For poems by: John Arden, Jim Burns, Johnny Byrne, Charles
Cameron, David Chaloner, John Cotton, Andrew Crozier, Dave
Cunliffe, Felix de Mendelssohn, Raymond Durgnat, Michael Hastings,
Geoffrey Hazard, Piero Heliczer, Pete Hoida, Michael Horovitz,
Libby Houston, Mark Hyatt, Roger Jones, David Kerrison, Seymour
King, David Kozubei, Herbert Lomas, Anna Lovell, Paul Matthews,
Michael McCafferty, John McGrath, Stuart Mills, Ted Milton, Tina
Morris, Neil Oram, Carlyle Reedy, Bernard Saint, Michael Shayer,
David Sladen, Tom Taylor, Alexander Trocchi, Patrick Waites,
Nicholas Snowden Willey, Bill Wyatt, and Michael X, thanks are
due to the authors.

Every effort has been made to trace copyright holders. The
publishers would be interested to hear from any copyright holders
not here acknowledged.

For the instances of their poetry quoted in the Commentary (and
in the Dedication), the Editor thanks Harry Fainlight, Allen Ginsberg
(and City Lights Books), Robert Gittings, Christopher Logue, and
William Blake.

*Books in the Penguin Modern Poets
are listed overleaf*

The Penguin Modern Poets

Not for sale in the U.S.A.
★Not for sale in the U.S.A. or Canada   †Available in the U.S.A.